# The New
# AIKIDO
# COMPLETE

**LYLE STUART INC.   SECAUCUS, NEW JERSEY**

# The New AIKIDO COMPLETE

## The Arts of Power and Movement

### BY YOSHIMITSU YAMADA

#### WITH STEVEN PIMSLER

First edition
Copyright © 1981 by Yoshimitsu Yamada

Queries regarding rights and permissions should be
addressed to: Lyle Stuart Inc., 120 Enterprise Ave.,
Secaucus, N.J. 07094.

Published by Lyle Stuart Inc.

In Canada: General Publishing Co. Limited,
Don Mills, Ontario.

Manufactured in the United States of America by
Halliday Lithograph, West Hanover, Mass.

Library of Congress Cataloging in Publication Data


Yamada, Yoshimitsu.
    The new Aikido complete.


    1.  Aikido.    I.   Pimsler, Steven, joint author.
I.  Title.
GV1114.35.Y355        796.8'154        80-21543
ISBN 0-8065-0301-2

I would like
to dedicate this book
to
*Professor Mitsunari Kanai,*
whose
knowledge, efforts, and
accomplishments have served
as an inspiration
toward the development
of
Aikido in the United States.

vi

# CONTENTS

# FOREWORD

I was given the opportunity to write *The New Aikido Complete* by my friend Lyle Stuart, who also published my first book. It has been almost ten years since *Aikido Complete* appeared. Since then, the art of Aikido has proliferated throughout the United States. It is being practiced and studied by increasing numbers of people from various lifestyles and professions.

Although there are several books available on Aikido whose authors are experts in the field, I felt that there was still a demand for a new instructional manual that would satisfy the needs of the the growing Aikido community in the United States. My experience with this enthusiastic group over the past fifteen years has enabled me to get to know them better, both as people and as Aikidoists. This has helped me to define their specific needs. Having devoted my entire career to teaching and spreading Aikido throughout the country, I have come into close daily contact with my students in all parts of the country. I have tried to listen to their questions, problems, and suggestions sensitively, to determine what will be helpful to their further development. This training guide is the result of my efforts to respond to their input in a practical way. I also hope that this book will help to introduce Aikido to those who have never seen it or had the opportunity to practice it.

The techniques shown in this book are basic ones, derived in part from the test requirements established by the United States Aikido Federation. It is impossible to introduce all Aikido techniques, owing to the very nature of the art itself. Aikido techniques are flexible, adapting to every kind of attack in a specific way. Therefore, the number of possible techniques is limitless. Those desiring more technical detail or philosophical depth are invited to consult some of the texts by such masters as Doshu Kisshomaru Ueshiba, the son of the founder of Aikido. I am merely presenting my small knowledge of Aikido concepts as a solid foundation upon which to build.

The reader will be able to get a better understanding of these basics through the photographs and illustrations. I believe this book to be unique, since all aspects of its creation were produced by people who are actively involved in the practice of Aikido.

I would like to express my personal appreciation to the various instructors I have studied under, especially Professor Kisshomaru Ueshiba, and to those people who have contributed to the successful completion of this book: Nobu Arakawa, who took the photographs; Lynn Sonneman, who drew the illustrations; Steven Pimsler, who assisted with the text; Peter Bernath, who designed the layout; and my three assistant instructors at the New York Aikikai, Angel Alvarez, Bruce Bookman, and Harvey Konigsberg, who appear as my "opponents" in the photographs.

YOSHIMITSU YAMADA

*Doshu Kisshomaru Ueshiba,*
*present leader of World Aikido.*

# The New
# AIKIDO
# COMPLETE

# About Morihei Ueshiba:
# The Founder of Aikido

*Morihei Ueshiba, founder of Aikido.*

The popularity of Aikido has grown tremendously in recent years, and one can find Aikido schools in almost every corner of the world. Introduced to the United States about twenty-five years ago, Aikido has enjoyed a sure and steady increase in the number of practitioners. In every Aikido *dojo* (school), one can observe the students bowing respectfully to a picture of an elderly gentleman with a wispy white beard and sparkling eyes that express a warm generosity. This gentleman is Master Morihei Ueshiba, the founder of Aikido, known to his students as O Sensei (Great Teacher). For those who wish to begin a serious study of Aikido, it is important to know something of his life and work before any clear understanding of the principles of Aikido is possible.

I was fortunate enough to study directly under O Sensei before I was sent to the United

States. Since the only way for one to see him now is through movies or pictures, we must pay close attention to the foundations of Aikido, which he developed, in order to get an accurate picture of the man. He was not only a great martial artist, but a warm and compassionate human being. I believe it is one of our goals in studying Aikido to emulate as much as possible his admirable characteristics.

The strength and depth of his character came from years of devotion to the pursuit of excellence and mastery in the many studies he undertook. Perhaps much of the determination that dictated the actions of O Sensei's life was a result of the many hardships he faced. His battles with sickness and personal tragedy were met with the same vigor he applied to pioneering new land settlements in northern Japan. But his most notable achievements were those forged on the frontiers of the martial arts.

From an early age he applied himself to the discipline of Japan's martial arts, known as *budo*. He became an accomplished master in several styles of ju jitsu, sword arts (kendo), and spear combat (sojitsu). The discoveries and experiments that led him to develop Aikido were based on a thoroughly expert foundation in the ways of fighting arts.

Mirroring his appetite for martial knowledge was the depth of his spiritual explorations. When he reached the plateau of excellence as a warrior, his religious beliefs put to the question the very nature of martial ways. He searched within himself to justify the validity of pursuing a course of life based upon the defeat of others. Such victories, he concluded, are merely relative and ultimately meaningless; there will always be someone bigger and stronger, so eventual defeat is inevitable. Each person is bound by his or her physical capabilities; but the potential for unlimited resources lies within the inner person. O Sensei understood that the real battle of life is to overcome the qualities of pettiness, ambition, and selfishness that keep our full potential from blossoming. At this point the unique aspect of his life's work began to take shape. He came to believe that the martial arts were to be used to purge one's character of these undesirable traits and ultimately to gain control of the entire self, both physically and mentally.

In developing the spiritual aspect of the martial arts he saw that budo should follow the laws of nature, be in harmony with them,

and serve to protect them. The object of his martial study would be to achieve a state of mind united with the universe itself. Therein would lie true strength. From this perspective O Sensei developed the arts of Aikido, a physical reflection of his spiritual beliefs.

The goals of Aikido are there for all to achieve. To become a person in harmony with others, to become an integrated and balanced individual, and to explore our full human potential should be the aims of the Aikido student. It is obviously a lifetime pursuit.

I hope that all the readers who practice the techniques I present will do so with the spirit of O Sensei's philosophy. This spirit is truly the heart of Aikido.

# The Nature of Aikido

When people see Aikido demonstrated, many different opinions emerge. Some say it is Zen in motion. To certain people the movement appears so graceful that it takes on a dancelike quality. Others remark that Aikido technique is very effective and deadly. A common viewpoint is that Aikido is beneficial for one's health because the body movement is natural, inducing calmness and relaxation.

Each of these opinions has a certain validity. However, Aikido is still a budo, a martial way. An often-used description of Aikido is that it is a "nonfighting art." This does not mean that one stays passive against attacks. On the contrary, Aikido is an outpouring of positive energy, and one must keep this in mind when practicing the art.

# Principles of Movement

The techniques of Aikido do not result in the conflict of opposing forces or the matching of power. The way in which Aikido employs power is what makes the techniques effective. Attacks are not stopped but are allowed to continue. Body movement is coordinated in such a way that the power of the Aikidoist is joined with the power of the attack, so that the Aikidoist becomes the controlling force for both powers. In this manner the force can be redirected harmlessly and harmoniously. The principle behind this is simple: Most attacks come in a straight line, whereas most Aikido movements are circular. The straight attack is drawn into the centrifigal force of the circular motion and thrown off, much like the effect of an object entering the field of a spinning top. We call this redirection of an attack "leading" the opponent's inner energy or intention.

For example, in the series of action photographs shown here, the Aikidoist takes the attack, which begins as a straight hand grab, and immediately moves to avoid the power of the attack. After the first turn, the Aikidoist joins with the attacker's momentum and leads the attacker around in a circle, controlling both the direction of movement and the balance of the attacker. At any given moment the Aikidoist can easily throw off the attacker and remain centered and balanced. (This particular technique is called *kaitenage.*)

In order to lead another person, we must first be able to lead ourselves. This type of mind-body control can occur only when the mind and body are relaxed and calm. This permits a clear perception of a situation. Repetition of technique builds up the body's reflexive responses so that when called upon to do so, the body will react spontaneously in a correct manner. A flexible, controlled body will adapt instantly to protect itself in a safe way.

These principles will become clearer as we go into the details of each technique.

# Etiquette

Etiquette is an important element in the practice of any form of budo. This is because of the serious nature of martial practice. Since your partner is not your competition, but rather the object of your practice, whenever we train in Aikido we bow to our partner in a proper manner to show respect and appreciation for her or him. Your partner is there to help you polish yourself; he or she is not to be defeated as an enemy.

## Proper Sitting (Seiza)

Photographs 1 and 1a show the proper sitting position. This is the way a student should sit when preparing for class. During that time she or he should do some form of relaxation or calming down, so that the mind may be clear to allow for correct practice. We say that a healthy mind and spirit belong to a proper posture; a strong mind is housed in a strong body. Photograph 2 shows an improper, unhealthy, and impolite way to sit.

When sitting, always keep your back straight, your shoulders relaxed and dropped, and your chin pulled in. Keep your knees a comfortable distance apart, not wider than your shoulder width and not closer than two fists apart. The tops of your feet should be on the ground, your buttocks sitting on your heels, with your big toes touching lightly. Place both hands on your thighs softly, palm down.

2

1

1a

9

# Proper Bowing (Rei)

From the proper sitting posture, picture 1, you are ready to bow. As is shown in picture 2, place the left hand down on the mat first, then the right hand, so that they form a triangle in front of you, as shown in picture 3. Keeping your back straight, lower your entire body to bow, as shown in picture 4. To return to a sitting position, place your right hand back to your thigh as shown in picture 5, then your left, and, once again keeping the back straight, return to your initial sitting posture.

When bowing to your partner, as seen in pictures 1a, 2a, and 3a, the mechanics of the simple bow are used. You must obviously also keep a proper distance between you so that you will not bump heads when you bow. More importantly, the distance is a reflection of your state of readiness for any action or necessary reaction that might occur even during the act of bowing.

2

1

3

4

1a

2a

5

3a

# Wrist Warm-ups

Needless to say, you must warm up before you begin your practice. There are no specific warm-up exercises except the ones I will present now, which are for the wrists. When you warm up it is important to take your time; otherwise, you may hurt yourself doing the exercises. Since each person has a different physical makeup, you must learn to keep your own pace during warm-up and stetching exercises.

In Aikido there are many techniques involving the joints of the body. Although they are not meant to go against the natural bend of the joints (as shown in picture 1), there is still some pain involved when the techniques are applied. Therefore, it is necessary to strengthen and loosen your wrists by doing the exercises shown. In this way they will become strong and flexible. You can see from illustrations 1, 2, and 3 the directions in which your power should be extended out when you are applying pressure to your wrist. In all the wrist exercises pressure is exerted by the last two fingers of the hand. It is very important not to become stiff or tense, especially in the shoulders, while you are applying pressure.

In pictures 2, 3, and 4, the way you hold your wrist is very important because it is exactly the way you will hold your partner's wrist in the technique called *kotegaeshi*. As you can see from illustration 2, you must keep the last two fingers of your hand exactly inside the wrist and close these fingers firmly at the same time that you are using the pressure from your thumb.

1

2

4

3

5

7

6

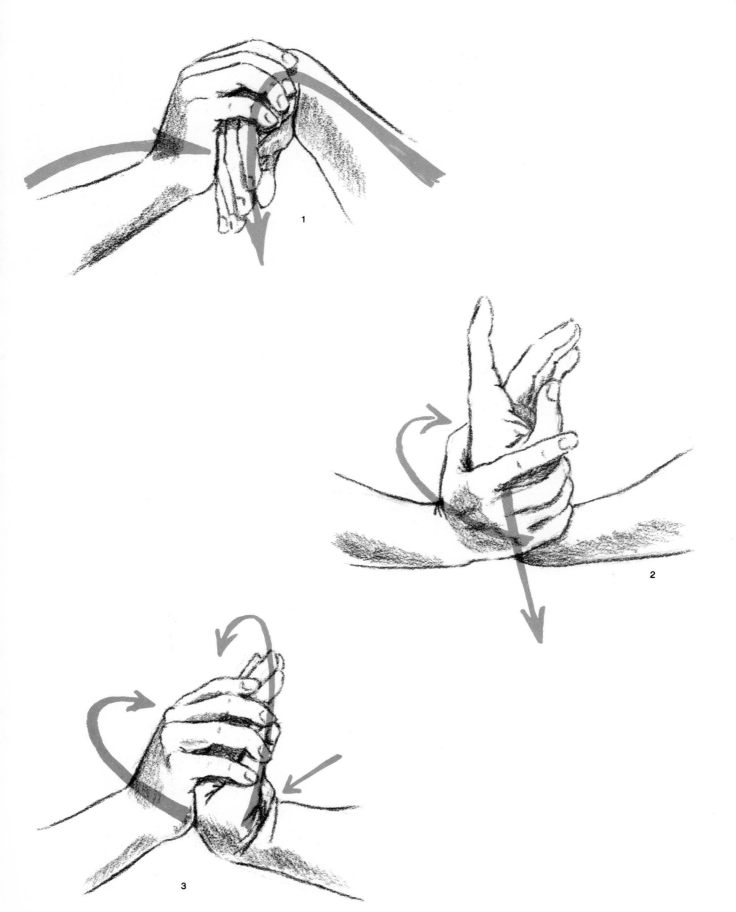

# Stance & Distance (Hanmi & Maai)

The proper stance in Aikido is called *hanmi*. Hanmi is a position that resembles a triangle. Picture 1 shows left hanmi (left foot forward), and picture 2 shows right hanmi (right foot forward). Hanmi provides a distinct advantage when defending movements are initiated. Refer to illustration 4 for the proper foot positions. Your feet should be a comfortable distance apart, about one and a half steps, with your weight evenly distributed. It is necessary in training that both *Nage* (person who is defending) and *Uke* (person who is attacking) keep a proper hanmi when beginning the techniques.

The distance between Uke and Nage is called *maai*. It is essential to keep the proper maai when practicing so that the techniques may be executed correctly. Usually the maai should be controlled by Nage. The maai shown in picture 3 is the ideal, common maai. In picture 4 you can see what happens with the incorrect maai.

When Uke and Nage are about to practice they must assume either a mutual hanmi or an opposite hanmi. When the hanmi is mutual, such as with both right feet forward, it is called *ai-hanmi*. When the stance is mutually opposite, such as when one partner has the right foot forward and the other partner the left, the hanmi is called *gyaku-hanmi*. Hanmi is largely determined by the technique being practiced. Always refer to the pictures for the correct starting hanmi so that you may follow the procedure easily.

1

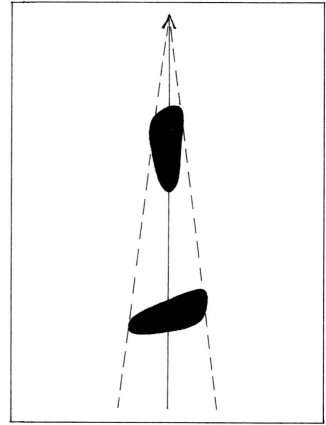

4

2

3

4

# Falling (Ukemi)

*Ukemi* is the first skill you must learn before attempting to learn any technique. It is the skill of falling safely. Ukemi doesn't mean defeat. I like to think of it as self-protection. By thinking of ukemi in that way you won't run the risk of becoming tense or stiff trying to recover from defeat. For this reason, beginners should devote a lot of time to practicing ukemi, either by themselves or with an advanced student to throw them.

Basically, there are two ways of falling in Aikido—a front roll or a back roll, depending on how one is thrown.

## Back Roll

As shown in pictures 1 and 2 you start the fall by drawing one leg behind you and placing the top of the foot against the mat, so that the sole of your foot faces up.

As you continue, as shown in picture 3, your whole left leg from knee to foot should be touching the mat. This is followed by sitting on the buttocks, as shown in picture 4. As this happens, keep your back round and your chin tucked in. As shown in picture 5, you focus your eyes on your belt knot so that you don't hit your head. Then try to bounce back up, as in pictures 6 and 7, reversing the order of falling down.

Pictures 8, 9, and 10 show how to fall back while receiving pressure from Nage. Always step back with the foot closest to Nage and try to carry your body in the direction of the pressure. If you step back with the wrong foot, as in picture 11, you will lose your balance, and your weight will go against the pressure you are receiving, causing pain in your joints.

1

2

4

6

5

7

8

10

9

11

# Front Roll

Start out in left hanmi, as shown in the series of pictures of the front roll. This means you will be rolling on your left side. When practicing front ukemi, you should always alternate sides to build up flexibility. Notice that during the entire roll the body is kept round and curved.

In pictures 1, 2, and 3, you bend down to begin your roll and you must make sure that you bend straight over so that your roll will be straight instead of on your side. Place your feet wide enough apart to facilitate a straight roll, as shown in illustrations 5, and 6. (In picture 4 you can see the wrong posture demonstrated, with the body all twisted up.)

In picture 2 and 3, you are about to commit yourself to the roll. Keep aiming your eyes to your back toes so that you don't go over head first when pushing off on your back foot. Be sure to keep your arm curved all through the roll. By pictures 7 and 8, you have completed your roll and should attempt to recover and stand up. At this point you must tuck your leg under you just as you did in the back roll. This will make it easier for you to recover.

In pictures 9 through 11, Uke is being thrown forward by Nage. Beginners can learn to roll easily from this exercise because they are not being held by Nage. Therefore, they are not forced to roll but are completely on their own. Uke can also get a good sense of cooperating with Nage's movement, even though Uke controls the roll. In pictures 9 and 10, with Uke standing in left hanmi, Nage puts his or her arm down, extending slightly forward. Uke's left arm should go down with Nage. Uke then steps forward on the right foot so the roll will be on the right side, as in picture 11. When stepping forward in this exercise Uke should take a big step forward and aim her or his arm and body straight ahead. Make sure your hand touches the mat before you begin to roll in this manner. Pictures 12 and 13 show a different angle of this front-roll exercise.

3

5

4

6

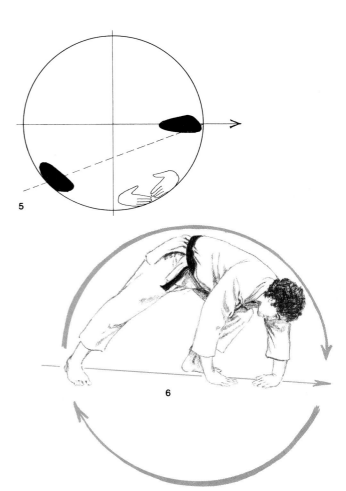

5

6

7

8

9

10

12

11

13

25

# Basic Movements

As I have stated and demonstrated previously, most Aikido techniques involve circular motion. However, there are two basic kinds of initial movements that are necessary before Nage attempts to lead Uke around. One is called *irimi* (an entering motion), and the other is called *tenkan* (a turning, or pivoting, motion).

## Irimi

For this basic irimi exercise Uke and Nage are in gyaku-hanmi. Nage starts in right hanmi, as in picture 1. Nage moves forward toward Uke, but not head on, or there will be a collision. As Nage starts moving in picture 2, the right arm is curved, joining Uke's arm in a parallel position. This puts Nage out of Uke's line of force. At the same time, Nage slides the right foot forward on a slight diagonal in order to move behind Uke. As this movement occurs Nage's left hand grabs Uke's wrist softly as shown in picture 3, stretching Uke's arm in the same direction as Uke's force, as shown in picture 4.

1

2

3

4

# Tenkan

This basic tenkan exercise starts in the same hanmi as the previous exercise, but in the initial movement Nage pivots on the right foot in order to avoid Uke's line of force. Before doing any footwork, Nage should bend the wrist that Uke is grabbing, in the same direction as Uke's power, as seen in picture 1. Nage's arm should be kept curved while doing this. Nage should be sure to keep his or her shoulders relaxed and extend energy out from her or his shoulders, down through the arm. This movement may require moving the right foot forward slightly, depending on the maai between Uke and Nage, as in picture 2. Nage then pivots on the right foot, swinging the left foot in the direction of the pivot, as in picture 3, resulting in a complete 180-degree turn. During this turning pivot Nage should keep a straight back and try to extend the right arm out, as he or she pivots. Nage's final position is again in right hanmi, as in picture 4.

1

2

3

4

# Back Stretch

This movement serves several pusposes: (1) to practice a basic irimi movement; (2) to help stretch Uke's back as part of a warm-up; and (3) to train Nage to keep her or his position and balance after the completion of a throw.

Uke and Nage start out in ai-hanmi. (Nage is in the right hanmi.) Uke grabs both of Nage's wrists with both of his hands. Nage moves the right foot diagonally forward, extending both arms in the same direction as shown in picture 1. In picture 2, Nage's left foot moves in front of his or her right foot as both hands are raised slightly above the head. Nage then pivots 180 degrees, without changing the position of her or his feet, as in picture 3. Gradually Nage lowers the extended arms and, as you can see in picture 4, is stretching Uke's back.

In order to support Uke's weight, Nage must bend slightly at the knees, keeping a straight back while extending both arms under Uke's neck. It is important that Nage maintain a fairly constant distance between his or her arms throughout the entire exercise.

1

2

3

# Kokyu-ho

One major difference between Aikido and the other martial arts is the way in which power is employed. In Aikido we extend our energy out instead of pulling it in, so the body doesn't have to become stiff or tense when we use power. We call this kind of extended power *kokyu ryoku*. There are two basic methods I like to use in training for this extended power.

## Sitting Kokyu-ho

The first method is done in a sitting position, as shown in picture 1. Please note that the purpose of this exercise is not to see whether Nage can throw Uke. It is strictly a means of training for power. Therefore, Uke's attitude in the exercise is important. Uke must consider the fact that she or he is mainly the object that receives and accepts Nage's extension, making it easy for Nage to do so. Uke's posture in picture 2 is improper because it is obviously not an accepting posture. The attitude here is rather competitive. If Uke's interest is in just defending against being dragged down to the mat, Nage can easily use a variety of methods to achieve that goal. As I stated before, the object of this exercise is not to throw Uke down; however, as a result of the proper extension of power, Uke will be thrown.

As Nage starts to extend his or her power, as in picture 3, it is important that Nage think of her or his energy as extending out in an unlimited way, beyond that of the immediate object in front of him or her.

Remember that the center and origin of one's energy is the stomach; let your energy keep emanating from this center throughout the exercise. Do not stop that energy at the shoulders, since this will make them stiff. Although this might appear to be a very strong posture, in reality Uke is receiving the sort of power that is mere muscular strength; it is not the proper extension of power originating from Nage's center of energy. Nage must keep all her or his power and energy flowing out through the shoulders, arms, and fingertips. Nage should also maintain the weight of his or her arm on its underside. This will make the arm heavy so that it curves itself naturally. Nage then tries to push forward toward Uke, not only from the arms but using the power of the entire body without getting up from the sitting position.

This method of using power is necessary in all Aikido techniques, especially when your body is in motion. Therefore, it is extremely important to understand the principle of maintaining your source of energy at your stomach. If you feel that your entire body comes up when you push Uke, then you are stopping your power at your shoulders.

At the end of this exercise, as shown in picture 6, Uke is on his or her back, and Nage is sitting on the heels, toes bent, weight settled back and centered. Nage should try to keep extending power out as shown by the arrows in illustration 7. At this point Uke may try to come straight up, in order to give Nage a feeling of extending power. Again this is not a situation where Uke tries every trick possible to sneak out from under Nage's pin; such actions serve no purpose in this exercise.

This particular skill is called kokyu-ho and the power generated by it is called kokyu-ryoku. Its general translation means "breath power." This means that the extension of power must be coordinated with the proper breathing. Obviously, if you intend to extend your power out it should be done when you exhale.

1

2

3

4

5

6

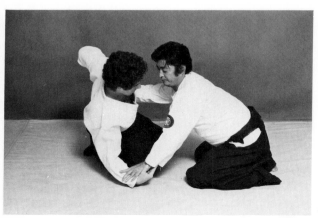

7

# Standing Kokyu-ho

This is the same skill and principle involved in sitting kokyu-ho, but both Uke and Nage are standing. In this training method Uke grabs Nage's right forearm with two hands. They are standing in gyaku-hanmi, as shown in pictures 1. This exercise will show how to extend power with body movement while altering the direction of power.

Nage first initiates an irimi movement toward Uke. In picture 2, it is necessary that Nage move her or his right foot slightly out of the way in order to advance the left foot, as shown in illustration 8. In picture 3, Nage's left foot approaches Uke, and this is the time Nage should extend his or her power, twisting the body in the same direction in which the right arm is extending. The position of Nage's arm and shoulder should be the same as in sitting kokyu-ho. Once again I must stress that it is not important whether you can throw Uke. The main point is whether you get a good position and break Uke's balance using a strong kokyu-ryoku, as seen in pictures 4 and 5.

Actually there are many ways to get Uke down once you have broken her or his balance.

In the next series of movements, Nage's hanmi is the same as in picture 6, but instead of initiating an irimi movement, Nage will use a tenkan movement. Before any body movement is attempted, Nage must try to extend power downward through the right arm as shown in picture 7. Then, in picture 8, Nage lowers his or her body by bending both knees deeply and completely in order to maintain balance. Nage stands straight up, as in picture 9, extending power upward as if lifting a heavy round object.

In this standing kokyu-ho exercise Uke may increase her or his holding power as both partners advance.

1

2

3

4

5

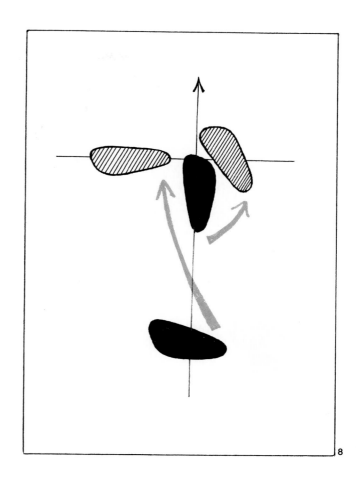

8

**6**

**8**

**7**

9

10

11    35

# Hand Positions

In the following series of pictures, you will be able to see how kokyu-ryoku is being utilized against various grabs through the position of the hands during the initial movement.

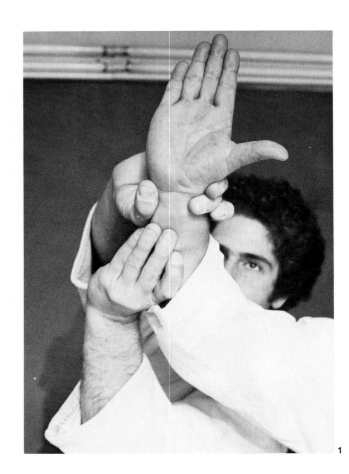

**3**

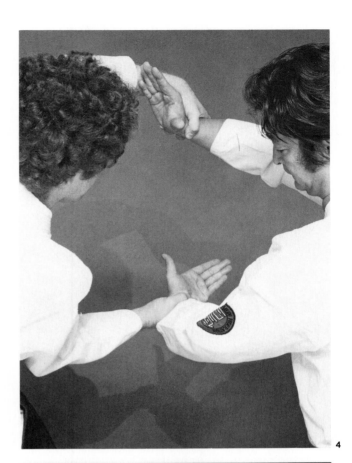

**4**

**5**

6

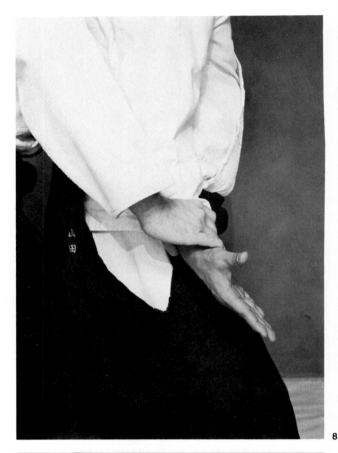

8

7

9

# Basic Irimi Nage

Now I'd like to present one of the basic techniques I always teach beginners. It gives them the feeling of Aikido movement as well as a sense of what it means to lead your opponent.

In picture 1, Uke and Nage are in ai-hanmi, Nage being in the right hanmi. Given this starting situation, no matter what Nage wants to do to Uke, Nage must resort to force. If Nage tries to pull Uke's arm without changing position, as in picture 2, obviously Uke will resist and pull back. If Nage pushes, it could result in the same conflict, since Uke may choose to push back. This happens because both Uke and Nage are in equally strong positions. However, if Nage moves behind Uke by stepping forward with the left foot, Nage will encounter no resistance or conflict as long as she or he continues to extend the arm as shown in picture 3. Now both Uke and Nage have their extensions going in the same direction, as in picture 4.

Remember that when Uke grabs Nage's wrist, no matter how strongly he or she may hold, Uke is grabbing only the wrist, not the whole body. Nage should not make the body stiff or tense, as if completely locked up; to do so will make him or her unable to move.

In picture 4 Nage is already behind Uke. Getting into this position is crucial in all Aikido techniques. We call this *shikaku*, which means the blind spot. This gives Nage a huge advantage for further movement. As a matter of fact, Nage has moved into the position of being the center of the circle and can lead Uke around. You can clearly see in illustration 9 the entire circle of movement and the positions of both Uke and Nage.

Since both Nage and Uke are facing the same direction, Nage is now in control and can easily lead Uke around and down. At this point Nage holds Uke's neck close into his right shoulder.

After having his balance broken by Nage's lead, Uke tries to regain balance, so Nage simply follows Uke's recovery, adding a kokyu-ryoku to throw Uke back. In pictures 5–7, Nage is lifting Uke's body up, as Uke is already doing. After this action, Nage moves the left foot diagonally to the left in order to maintain better balance and to make room for the final movement. Then Nage slides the right foot diagonally forward with the conclusion of his or her arm extension, as in picture 8, throwing Uke down in picture 9. When he or she is finally thrown, Uke should take a back

roll tucking the foot closest to Nage (the right foot in this case) behind him or her.

Since the purpose of this technique is to give Nage the idea of the circular nature of Aikido movements, and since Nage may be a beginner, Uke should have an attitude of helping Nage. Uke does this by keeping her or his attention focused on the attack of Nage's wrist and by following Nage's lead so that Nage can get a clear, continuous feeling of the entire movement. If Uke changes her or his mind or changes the attack, it will be very difficult for Nage to complete the technique.

When both partners become advanced, Nage should be able to complete the throw or change the technique despite a change in the direction of Uke's attack.

1

2

3

4

5

6

9

7

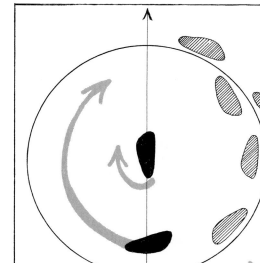

9

8

# Knee-Walking (Shikko)

As we advance in Aikido, we often practice almost all the techniques in a sitting position, as well as standing. The purpose of doing this is to make your lower body strong; this will then facilitate practicing the techniques when you are standing.

The following series of pictures shows the basic way to advance in the sitting position called *suwari waza*. When starting, lift up one knee to move forward, as shown in picture 2. Make sure to bring the heel of the back foot to meet the heel of the forward foot. It is as if your feet were tied together in a perpendicular position at the ankles. During the entire movement your weight should not be on the knees but should be evenly balanced between the knees as in the normal sitting position. If you don't keep your weight balanced on your heels you will run the risk of injuring your knees, and your movement will become clumsy and slow. Try not to think that you are advancing on your knees but rather that you are moving from your center of energy, the abdominal area. It is also important that you keep your toes bent under you throughout the movement. The practice of suwari waza should really be done under the guidance of an experienced practitioner, in order to avoid injury.

1

2

3

5

4

6

43

Attacks &
Techniques

# Atemi Waza

At certain times in the description of techniques I will mention opportunities for Nage to deliver strikes, or *atemi*. The public always has questions concerning atemi in Aikido techniques, and that is one reason I have chosen to demonstrate certain atemi. The other reason is to give the reader examples of the opportunities that exist to apply atemi if desired. Atemi can also be used to help Nage check to see if he or she is in a strong, balanced position during the entire course of a technique. In this way, Nage is able to deliver an aggressive counterattack should that be necessary.

Usually in our daily practice we do not often employ atemi, because if Nage concentrates on the atemi movements, she or he might lose the continuity required to feel the technique properly.

# Shomenuchi

## The Attack

In the shomenuchi attack, Uke is applying a straight strike aiming at Nage's forhead, as shown in picture 1.

# Shomenuchi Irimi Nage

In order that beginners may avoid confusion in this technique, both partners should stand in ai-hanmi. This will allow them to get the movement right. In the following pictures, Nage and Uke are in right hanmi.

The footwork in this technique is exactly the same as that shown in the basic irimi nage. The difference is that in this attack Nage must avoid Uke's striking power instead of dealing with a simple hand grab.

As Uke's striking hand is about to approach in picture 1, Nage gets out of Uke's line of force by raising the right arm and extending it forward. In all cases, the extension of the arm is done in the same fashion as in kokyu-ho, with the arm curved and the power originating from one's center of energy. It may appear that Nage is blocking or receiving the power of Uke's strike, but actually, by extending ko-kyu-ryoku, Nage is already in the process of moving out of Uke's line of force, as in picture 2. Since Nage is moving into shikaku, the blind spot, he or she is able to deliver atemi as shown in picture 3. Having extended the right arm, Nage is able to move behind Uke into shikaku, as shown in picture 4. Picture 4a shows the same position of avoiding Uke's strike from a different angle.

As soon as Nage is in shikaku, she or he must cut down Uke's strike using the right arm like the blade of a sword. At the same time this cut is being made, Nage's left hand brings Uke's neck to the right shoulder in the same direction as the cut down. In the third simultaneous action in this movement, Nage must draw his or her right leg back in order to get into the positions shown in pictures 5 and 5a. To recap all three steps: Nage cuts down Uke's right arm, draws the right foot back, and brings Uke's neck to the right shoulder. As shown in picture 6, Nage is again in a position to deliver atemi.

Once in this position, Uke attempts to regain balance. Nage, holding Uke's neck securely to her or his right shoulder, raises her or his curved right arm, extending power upward, and follows Uke's attempt to stand up, as in picture 7. When Nage is in the position shown in illustration 10, he or she must move the left foot slightly to the left to make room for the next movement. Pictures 8 and 8a are the completed positions after Nage brings Uke up.

Since Uke is off-balance, Nage just has to slide the right foot diagonally forward, extending the right arm toward the ground in order to complete the throw as shown in pictures 9, 9a, and 9b. After completing the throw, Nage should maintain a strong, balanced postion in the correct hanmi, as in picture 10.

There is a very important element in the initial movement of this technique, which goes along with the physical mechanics of the technique. The mental attitude of Nage is critical here, because he or she is dealing with a striking attack. If Nage is afraid of the strike it will make her or his entire body stiff, so that she or he will not even be able to execute the smallest footwork. Nage must stand confidently, keeping his or her body relaxed and calm. If Nage can achieve this he or she will be able to do any variety of initial movements to avoid Uke's attack. This strong positive mental attitude serves as the basis for beginning all Aikido techniques.

1

2

3

4

4a

5

5a

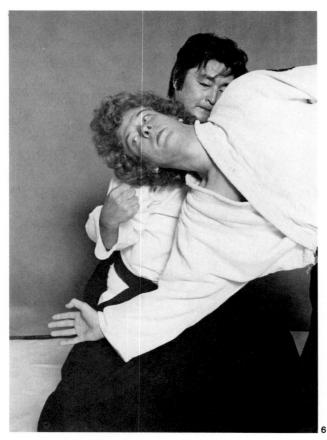

6

8a

9

7

9a

8

9b

10

10

51

# Shomenuchi Ikkyo

## Omote Variation

Many techniques in Aikido can be done using either an irimi (entering) or a tenkan (turning) motion. When a technique uses an irimi motion it is called *omote*. When a tenkan motion is employed, the technique is called *ura*.

The technique called shomenuchi ikkyo is divided into these two variations. First I will explain the omote variation.

The purpose of applying ikkyo is to put your opponent down to the ground, employing one hand to grab the wrist and the other to hold the elbow while applying downward power. Ikkyo uses no pressure against the joints. In the next series of photographs Nage is applying ikkyo against Uke's shomenuchi attack. Nage's mental attitude at the beginning of the technique should be the same as was detailed in shomenuchi irimi nage. Both partners again start in ai-hanmi.

As Uke's strike comes, Nage raises both arms simultaneously, extending them with kokyu power, as shown in picture 1. The direction of Nage's movement is forward, as opposed to turning behind Uke as in irimi nage. Although the direction is forward, Nage's focus should be slightly on the diagonal, in this case to the right. As Nage raises her or his arms, her or his right foot advances slightly to the right so that at the point of contact with Uke's arm, Nage can use the twisting power of the entire body to bring Uke's arm down.

In picture 2, Nage is about to meet Uke's strike. The blade of Nage's right hand meets Uke's wrist, while the left hand comes under Uke's elbow, catching it between the thumb and the index finger. At this point Nage must be sure to move the right foot out diagonally, so that his or her body is facing the proper direction. This makes it possible to keep both Nage's arms and Uke's arm extended and in front of Nage's body, as seen in picture 3. From that point Nage pushes Uke's arm up but only as far as the extension will allow, as in picture 4. (Picture 4a shows this at a different angle.) Do not overreach; that will cause Nage to loose balance. Nage's feet must always be firmly planted on the ground.

After reaching the correct upward extension, Nage begins to press Uke's arm down, inscribing a complete circle with Uke's elbow in front of Uke's face. At the same time, Nage's left foot advances forward deeply, breaking Uke's balance, as in pictures 5 and 5a. From there Nage simply takes another step forward with the right foot, as in picture 6, exerting pressure down on Uke's elbow, as seen in picture 7. At the final position, with Uke face down on the ground and Nage in a sitting posture (picture 8), Nage brings his or her left knee to Uke's armpit, firmly grasping the elbow with his or her left hand and Uke's wrist with his or her right, in the same manner in which Uke was brought down. (See picture 9.) Remember, no wrist lock or arm lock is involved in the ikkyo finish, merely the continuation of Nage's extended power.

The crucial point in this technique is found in picture 2. Nage should not be grabbing Uke's arm at this time because it is very difficult to catch the arm from a powerful strike such as shomenuchi. Even if Nage does catch the arm, her or his entire movement, along with her or his extension, will be stopped there. Instead, Nage should meet Uke's arm without grabbing it, pushing through so that he or she can continue the extension. In this way, Nage will be able to put Uke down in one motion.

1

4a

2

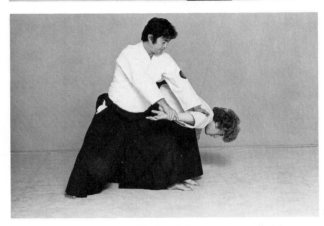

5

3

5a

4

6

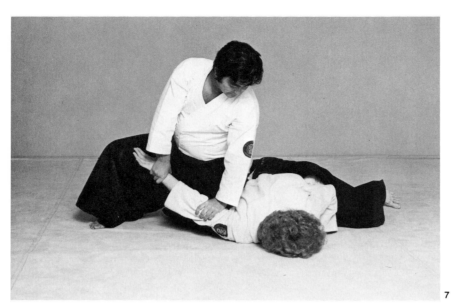

7

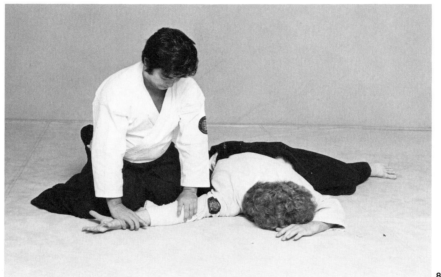

8

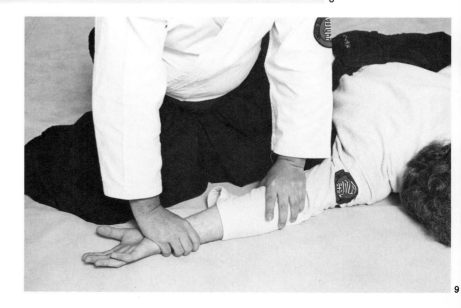

9

# Shomenuchi Ikkyo

## Ura Variation

In order to apply ikkyo ura, Nage must position herself or himself in Uke's shikaku. As Nage extends both arms to meet Uke's strike, as in picture 1, he or she moves the left foot behind Uke's right foot, as in picture 2. As Nage does so, the arms' extension should be the same as in the omote movement. Please notice the difference in the initial step between the omote and ura ikkyo: in omote, Nage advances forward with the right foot toward Uke; In ura, Nage moves the left foot behind Uke.

Picture 2 indicates the proper postion after Nage makes the first step for ura. From that postion Nage swings the right foot around, pivoting on the left foot while bringing his or her arms and Uke's arm down simultaneously, as in picture 3. Nage should continue that swinging, turning motion until Uke is on the ground, as in pictures 4, 5, and 6. During Nage's entire swinging motion she or he must always keep Uke's arm extended and in front of her or him, with the pressure on Uke's elbow being downward as shown in illustration 11. It is important that Nage keep both arms equally extended in order to apply equal pressure to Uke's arm. One thing to avoid is pulling Uke's arm as Nage swings around. Please remember that your purpose is to bring Uke down, so the power from your arms should be downward during the entire circular motion.

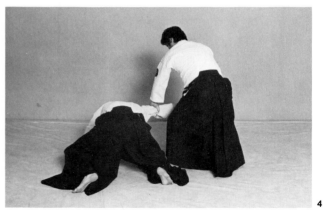

5

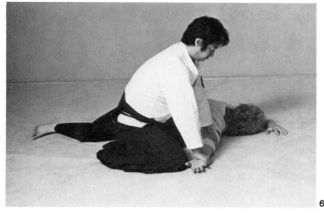

6

11

# Shomenuchi Sankyo

Nage's initial movement in shomenuchi sankyo is exactly the same as in shomenuchi ikkyo omote. After Nage completes the ikkyo technique as shown in picture 4, he or she must switch the left hand in order to grab Uke's right wrist, as in pictures 5 and 6. Picture 7 shows the completion of switching the hands for the sankyo technique. Once Nage holds Uke's hand in the sankyo, refer to illustration #12 for the proper application of pressure. Nage must make sure to close the last three fingers of her or his hand strongly, with, Nage's thumb covering the base of Uke's thumb. Nage should not lose that grip until the completion of the entire movement.

Pictures 8 through 11a show Nage bringing Uke down. In picture 8 you can see how Nage changes position while putting her or his right hand on uke's elbow. After Nage changes position completely as in picture 9, he or she simply moves backward until Uke is down on the ground. Remember that the pressure on Uke's elbow should be downward all the way.

Picture 11a is another view of the position of picture 11, which shows clearly what the final pin should look like. From picture 12, you can see that Nage's right hand, which was on Uke's elbow, slides up to replace her or his left hand while still applying a sankyo twist. Nage then moves the left hand to hold Uke's elbow against Nage's body for the final pin, as in picture 13.

4

5

6

7

8

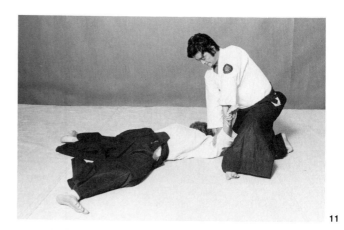

11

11a

9

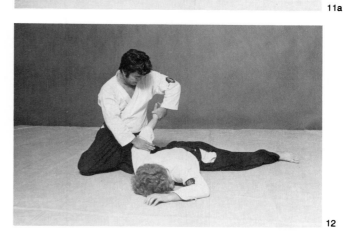

12

10

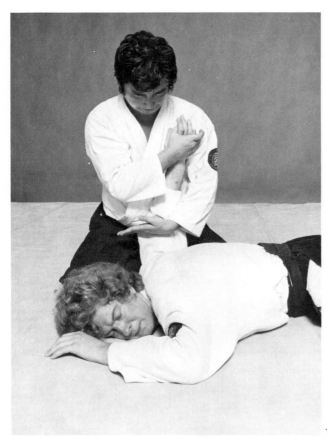

13

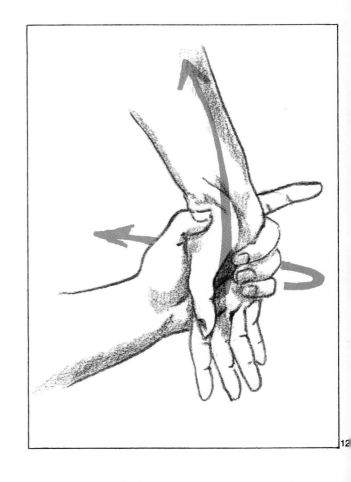

12

# Yokomenuchi

## The Attack

In the yokomenuchi attack, Uke strikes at the side of Nage's head, as shown in picture 1. Before the strike Uke and Nage stand in ai-hanmi. When Uke delivers the attack, she or he steps forward with the back foot so that the attack is in gyaku-hanmi. Uke is in effect striking at the side of Nage closest to him or her.

It is important to realize that when Nage initiates this technique, the approaching motion is already forming a circular pattern. Whenever Nage makes this movement, she or he must consider that Uke has immediately become part of the circular pattern as well.

# Yokomenuchi Irimi Nage

I have demonstrated three different types of irimi nage from the yokomenuchi attack. They are called (a), (b), and (c).

## Technique (a)

No matter what kind of technique is applied against this attack, the most crucial part is going to be Nage's initial movement. There are basically two opening movements that can be used. In this technique Nage is using a movement that lets Uke complete the attack by moving out of his or her original position. Let me explain the footwork of Nage's initial movement first.

Since Uke's movement is already circular, Nage's first foot movement is to move the back foot (the right foot in this case) to the right side, as seen in pictures 1, 2, and 3. Almost at the same time that Nage's weight shifts to the right foot, Nage pivots on that foot slightly, bringing the left foot back. During this part of the footwork, Nage must raise the left hand fully extended, not to block, but rather to lead Uke's striking arm down (or let Uke complete the attack). At the same time the right hand may be used to deliver atemi, as shown in picture 4.

At this point in the technique it is important that Nage not attempt to catch Uke's arm when it is striking, for several reasons: (1) it is impossible to catch; (2) Nage will receive all of Uke's power; and (3) Nage's movement will be stopped. In order to apply various techniques, the right hand should really move down in the same direction as the left arm. Ideally, this right hand should come down under Uke's attacking arm so that at the end of this movement Uke's hand should be sandwiched between Nage's hands. At this point Nage grabs Uke's wrist with the right hand. Remember that the footwork and arm motions are occurring at the same time so that the effect is of one motion.

I mentioned before that as Nage pivots on the right foot, she or he shouldn't turn too much. Nage's position after this pivot should be one of facing Uke in hanmi. If Nage pivots too severely, he or she will wind up with his or her back to Uke. Picture 5 shows Nage in the proper position after the initial movement.

From this position Nage can move in any direction, according to Uke's next reaction. Once again, if Nage pivots too much, she or he cannot move freely at all. Please remember that it is important to make the correct initial movement against any attack before you attempt to apply any technique. *The technique always comes after the proper initial movement.* Needless to say, once the proper opening is executed, the technique is easier to apply.

In pictures 6 and 6a, Nage is about to go into the irimi nage technique, moving in behind Uke. Nage should stretch out his or her right arm, also serving to stretch out Uke's arm. This will make it easier to move behind Uke. The rest of the movement, as shown in pictures 7 through 11, is based on the basic irimi nage. The difference here, however, is that in this technique Nage is holding Uke's wrist, whereas in the basic irimi nage, Uke is grabbing Nage's wrist. It may happen that Nage decides to become aggressive and try to pull Uke's arm. Please don't fall into this kind of thinking but continue to extend your arm while leading Uke, the same as you would do if Uke were grabbing. *In Aikido techniques the general rule is to extend, not to pull.*

3

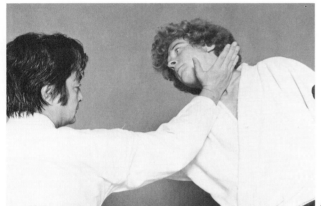

4

6a

5

6

7

8

10

9

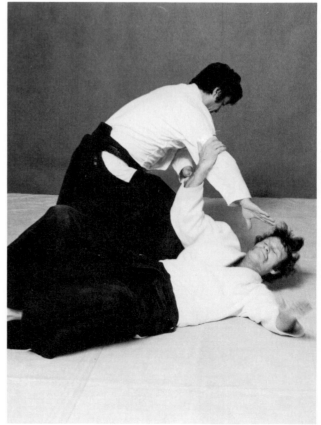

11

# Technique (b)

In this technique Nage is making a different initial movement. This movement goes diagonally toward Uke's attack. As soon as Uke is in the process of attacking, Nage advances by sliding her or his front foot (the left foot in this case) forward; then the right foot follows, as in picture 2. As Nage slides in, he or she extends his or her arm, with the intention not of blocking, but of extending beyond Uke's arm. Ideally, the place Nage should be aiming for is in the area around Uke's elbow, as in picture 3. Needless to say, Nage's entering motion should be deep, the deeper the better. In this way Uke's balance is broken. In picture 4, Nage is cutting down with the left hand and at the same time steps to the right with the right foot. By this time Nage's right arm should be in the same position as in the previous irimi nage, picture 5. Picture 6 shows the completed throw.

3

4

1

5

2

6

65

## Technique (c)

In this technique Nage makes the same initial movement as in irimi nage (b). However, Nage is not able to move in deep enough to accomplish the previous technique. As seen in picture 3, Nage's position is not as deep as in technique (b), so Uke's striking arm is maintained at Nage's eye level. In pictures 4 and 5, Nage is moving out from under Uke's attack, curving the left arm much more sharply than has previously been done. This forces Uke's attacking arm to slide down. Meanwhile, Nage uses the right arm as a blade to help cut down Uke's arm, as in picture 6. While Nage is performing this cutting motion her or his entire body must move behind Uke into shikaku. In picture 7, Nage's position is in shikaku, exactly as was demonstrated in the shomenuchi irimi nage. The rest of the movement, as seen in pictures 8, 9, and 10, follows suit.

The crucial point of this technique is in the initial movement, as Nage enters. Nage must be sure to enter diagonally instead of straight toward Uke's body. From that position Nage ends up clearly being able to see Uke's reaction, especially Uke's left arm. Also important to Nage's entering motion is for Nage to keep the weight of her or his body down low. Nage should not try to raise her or his body to meet Uke's strike. This would weaken Nage's balance. In this case Nage doesn't have to come up to meet Uke's attack, since Uke is already coming at Nage.

1

2

3

4

5

6

7

8

9

10

# Yokomenuchi Shihonage (Omote)

In yokomenuchi shihonage, the initial movement will be the same as in irimi nage (a), where Uke's attack is allowed to complete itself. In pictures 2, 2a, 3, and 3a, the initial movement can be seen from various angles. After the completion of the opening movement (picture 4) Nage is going to apply shihonage. As was mentioned in irimi nage (a), Uke's right hand becomes sandwiched between Nage's hands. In this case both hands grasp Uke's hand, as shown in illustration 13, with the right hand gripping strongly.

From this position Nage stretches Uke's arm widely, making a wide step to the right with the right foot, as shown in picture 5. At this point Nage should bring both arms up, making room for himself or herself to step through. Next, Nage steps forward with the left foot and as soon as the left toes touch the ground, Nage pivots completely, bringing Uke's arm above Nage's head, as in pictures 6 and 7. When the pivot is complete, both Uke's and Nage's arms should end up in front of Nage's center, as shown in picture 8.

From this position Nage continues the downward swing of her or his arms, moving forward slightly with the right foot as in picture 9. From picture 5, as Nage moves into shihonage, Nage can deliver atemi, as shown in picture 10.

More details on how to apply shihonage will follow in the chapter dealing with techniques in katatetori, because it will be easier to see the fine points when a simple hand grab is

2

2a

3

1

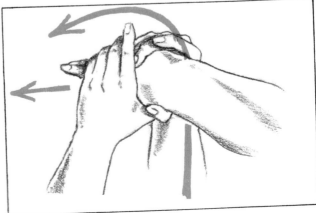

13

3a

7

4

8

5

9

6

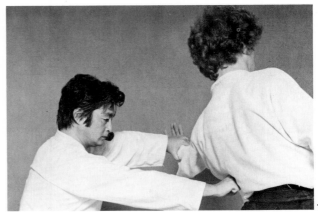

10

69

# Yokomenuchi Gokkyo

In this demonstration, Nage will initiate an irimi movement, but as in irimi nage (c), Nage is again not able to enter deep enough to bring Uke's arm down. Once again, both Uke's and Nage's arms will remain at eye level in front of Nage, as in picture 3.

After Nage enters, instead of using the right hand as a blade, Nage's right hand grabs Uke's wrist, as shown in the close-up, picture 4. As soon as he or she grabs Uke's wrist, Nage moves the left hand to grab Uke's elbow (picture 5), bringing his or her body into shikaku. Nage then brings Uke's arm down in the same manner as shown in shomenuchi ikkyo omote (pictures 6 through 9).

Since this technique is applied against Uke while she or he is holding a weapon, usually a knife, Nage must exert pressure against Uke's wrist, as shown in pictures 10 and 11, in order to take the weapon away.

2

3

4

1

70

5

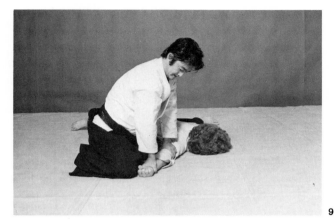

9

6

10

7

8

11

# Tsuki

## The Attack

The tsuki attack is a straight punch, as seen in picture 1. It may be a punch to the face or to the belly. The following series of techniques are against tsuki to the belly. However, the same techniques can be applied to either attack. Pictures 2 through 5 show the proper way to deliver a tsuki attack.

1

2

3

4

5

# Tsuki Kotegaeshi

In this technique Nage's hanmi is not important in being able to apply the kotegaeshi. For this demonstration, however, Nage will stand in the left hanmi against a right-handed attack by Uke in order to show the basic movements clearly (pictures 1 and 1a). As in other Aikido techniques, Nage doesn't stand in his or her original position and wait for the attack; rather, Nage makes an irimi movement so as to put himself or herself in Uke's shikaku.

In pictures 2 and 2a, Nage is making the entering movement, sliding the left foot diagonally forward to avoid Uke's line of attack. As the irimi motion occurs, Nage uses the left hand to push away or guide Uke's tsuki in the direction the punch is going (refer to pictures 7 and 7a). Nage must not attempt to block the punch because if he does, it will most likely cause Uke to react with the left hand.

In picture 3, Nage is in Uke's shikaku, holding Uke's wrist. Nage is grabbing the wrist as a result of the completion of the initial irimi movement. Nage should not grab the wrist first; if Nage decides to grab the wrist at the beginning, she or he will sometimes find herself or himself directly in Uke's line of attack. Perhaps, with luck, Nage will get the wrist; if not, unfortunately, Uke will have an opportunity to make another attack easily.

As soon as Nage grabs the wrist, he or she, should extend the left arm and bring it slightly downward as Nage draws the right foot back (picture 4). Nage must make the extension continous, bringing Uke around to Nage's right. This movement will break Uke's balance completely, as seen in picture 5. In picture 6, Nage is about to apply the kotegaeshi technique. Nage holds Uke's wrist in the same manner as is shown in the kotegaeshi wrist warm-up. Nage's bottom two fingers are held tight around the inside of Uke's wrist, while the thumb serves as the guide for the direction of the twist (see illustration 14). As Nage puts pressure on Uke's wrist Nage draws the left foot back (pictures 7 and 8). During this entire movement Nage should keep Uke's wrist in front of Nage's body, extending both arms.

Pictures 9 through 13 show the conclusion of the technique. Throughout the finish Nage's left hand maintains the kotegaeshi grip.

The crucial part of this technique leading your uke or keeping him moving around you as soon as you enter in shikaku and grab the wrist.

1

1a

2

2a

3

6

7

4

8

5

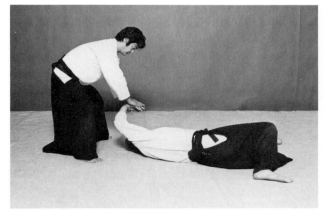

9

10

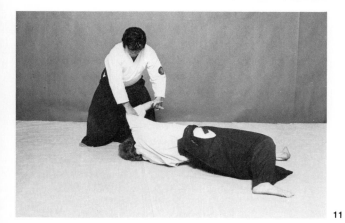

11

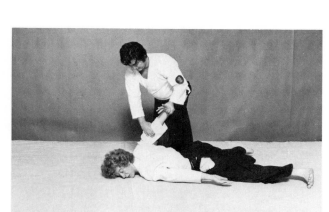

12

13

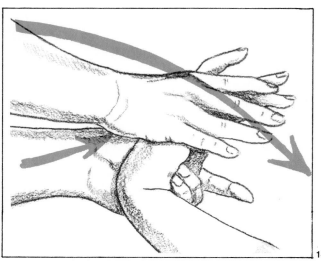

14

# Tsuki Irimi Nage

In the last technique the movement was a combination of irimi and tenkan motion. In this technique Nage's movement is strictly irimi.

As Uke's attack comes, Nage once again slides the left foot diagonally forward (picture 1). As Nage does so, he or she uses the left hand to lead Uke's punch down, as in pictures 2 and 3. In picture 4, Nage then uses the right arm in the same manner as shown in the basic irimi nage. At the same time, Nage steps forward on the right foot to complete the throw, as shown in pictures 5, 6, and 7. (Pictures 1a through 6a show the technique from a different angle.)

As Nage enters initially, she or he may deliver atemi as is shown in picture 8.

3

4

1

5

2

6

7

4a

1a

5a

2a

6a

3a

8

77

# Katetetori

## The Attack

Picture 1 shows the proper way for Uke to grab Nage's wrist in the katatetori attack.

# Katatetori Shihonage (Omote)

In this technique, when Uke grabs Nage's wrist, Nage must expect a further attack from Uke, as shown in pictures 1 and 1a. Uke is not just holding the hand and standing still.

In pictures 2 and 2a, Nage is moving out of Uke's line of attack by switching hanmi and the direction of movement. Nage does this by drawing back the left foot as she or he advances the right foot on a slight diagonal to the right. Both steps occur simultaneously. At the same time, Nage should extend his or her power strongly, using the rising curve of his or her left arm, pointing the fingers upward. As Nage's arm spirals up almost to Uke's eye level (as shown in picture 3), Nage grabs Uke's wrist firmly with the right hand. Even after Nage grabs Uke's wrist with the right hand, Nage should continue to keep the left hand extended, because the rest of her or his movement will follow the direction in which her or his left fingertips are pointing.

In picture 4, Nage brings the left foot forward while bringing both arms and Uke's arm up. Everything should be kept in front of Nage. In pictures 5 and 6, after Nage advances the left foot, he or she pivots in the direction the left fingers are pointing.

The pivot must be a complete 180-degree swivel of the body, as shown in the picture. Nage then swings her or his arms down, fully extending them in order to bring Uke down, as in picture 8.

1

1a

2

2a

3

4

7

5

8

6

# Shihonage (Ura)

In this demonstration Nage applies the shihonage using a tenkan movement at the beginning.

Nage makes a tenkan movement to avoid Uke's line of attack. Nage must slide the left foot forward slightly, however, in order to get a better position for the tenkan, as shown in pictures 2 and 2a. Please notice that when Nage's right hand is about to grab Uke's wrist, her or his left hand is in the same curved extension as in shihonage omote. (Pictures 3, 3a, and 3b show a different angle of this tenkan.) You should also note that Nage's left arm and Uke's right arm are parallel and going in the same direction.

After Nage completes the tenkan, she or he pivots all the way, swinging both arms widely over her or his head until she or he gets into the position shown in picture 6. Nage then completes the shihonage as in the omote movement (picture 7).

1

2

2a

3

4

3a

4a

3b

5

5a

6a

6

7

# Katatetori Kokyu Nage

Beginners can also use this technique to help them practice their front rolls. Nage may use his or her position shown in picture 4 to apply many other techniques, such as kaitenage, which was shown on pages 7 and 8.

As soon as Uke grabs Nage's wrist, Nage advances the right foot diagonally forward while lifting the right arm, as in picture 2. At the same time, Nage uses the left hand for atemi. This initial motion must be done immediately, before Uke can make any attack after grabbing.

In picture 2, Nage has raised the right arm high enough so that there is enough room for him to go under Uke's arm. He advances with the left foot and then pivots, as shown in picture 3. From there Nage extends his arm down, stepping forward on the right foot to let Uke roll forward (pictures 5 and 6).

Again the crucial part of this technique is to get into the position in picture 4. Needless to say, Nage should make his or her right arm extremely strong, giving full extension throughout the entire movement.

# Ryotetori

## The Attack

In the ryotetori attack, Uke grabs both of Nage's wrists in both hands, as shown in picture 1.

# Ryotetori Tenchi Nage

Uke and Nage stand in gyaku-hanmi, with Nage in the left hanmi (picture 1). This technique's name is descriptive of the movements—*ten* means sky, and *chi* means ground. As in the meaning of the name, Nage's one hand (the left hand in this case) is extended downward while the other is aiming up.

Nage must do three things simultaneously in the initial movment: (1) slide his or her foot diagonally to the side of Uke's forward foot; (2) extend his or her left hand downward, in the same direction as the left foot; and (3) point his or her right hand upward, keeping the elbow down. Nage should keep his or her right hand on the inside of Uke's wrist. If this hand is on the outside, as shown in illustration 15, Nage's body cannot move forward because she or he receives Uke's power and resistance. As long as Nage's right hand is set inside Uke's wrist, Nage can move freely without resistance.

I have shown three different angles of the initial movement in pictures 2, 2a, and 2b. Notice that Nage's left hand is strongly extended down and he keeps it down until he completes the throw. Also notice that Nage's weight is kept down.

In pictures 3, 3a, and 3b, you can see Nage raising his right arm in a circular pattern in order to bring Uke up. He continues this curve in betweeen Uke's shoulder and face. As the right hand moves in its arc, Nage advances his right foot forward on a slight diagonal (pictures 4, 4a, and 4b). Nage should make sure that Uke's balance is broken before she or he steps with the right foot (picture 5).

As I mentioned before, Nage should keep extending her or his left hand down. It can easily happen that Nage forgets to keep extending the left hand when he or she starts to use the right hand.

In order to maintain a strong balance, Nage must make sure that she or he slides the left foot forward in the initial movement, moving on a diagonal and keeping the left foot pointing out towards the left before making the final step (picture 4b).

15

2

2a

2b     87

3

3a

3b

4

4a

4b

5

# Ryotetori Irimi Nage

In the initial movement for this technique, Nage moves his or her right foot out to the right side, as in picture 2. Nage does this in order to move out of the line of attack and also to make room for her or his left foot to approach (picture 3). As Nage makes the approaching step with the left foot (which is also a kind of cross step in front of the right foot), he or she curves the right arm so as to join with the shape of Uke's arm.

In the approaching process, as seen in pictures 3 through 5, Nage should not look at Uke but instead should face in the same direction in which his or her body is turning. If Nage looks at Uke it will cause a collision and make Uke's intention in the movement stop.

As Nage begins this curving motion (picture 4), he or she is going to make a complete circle with the right arm as his or her right foot and entire body slide next to Uke's side. Nage should not slide to uke's side until she or he completes the circular movement of the right arm (picture 5). The arm should be on its way down as Nage slides in, and Uke's body should be bent over as a result of this downward movement, causing Uke to lose balance, as in picture 7. Nage's left hand remains in the same position throughout the technique.

5

8

6

9

7

# Morotetori

## The Attack

In the morotetori attack, Uke grabs Nage's forearm with both hands, as picture 1 shows.

# Morotetori Irimi Nage

In all the techniques against the morotetori attack, Nage's initial movement requires the same kind of body coordination that is explained in the section on kokyu-ho (pages 30 to 31) and shown here in pictures 1 and 2.

In picture 3, Nage moves the right hand and foot to his right side, also shown by the arrows in illustration 16. Nage can apply atemi at this position, as shown in picture 4. In picture 5, Nage keeps bringing his right arm down and simultaneously brings his left foot behind Uke. Once he gets there, he is in Uke's shikaku, so that the following movements will be exactly the same as in basic irimi nage (pictures 6 through 9).

The crucial point in this technique is when Nage makes the reversal motion, as seen in illustration 16. Nage needs to swing his or her arm in a complete circle, bringing Uke around in order to get Uke off-balance. Nage's arm motion changes the direction Uke is going in by using this circular movement.

93

5

9

6

7

8

16

# Morotetori Nikkyo

Nage uses the exact same opening movement used in the previous technique. She or he simply applies the nikkyo technique (a form of pressure on the wrist) at the point in which she or he completes the reverse motion, as in the previous irimi nage (picture 3). This is done before Nage would step behind Uke. The detail of the direction of pressure in the nikkyo technique is best shown in the close-up, picture 8, on page 96.

5

6

7

8

# Katatori

## The Attack

In the katatori attack, as shown in picture 1, Uke grabs Nage's sleeve in the shoulder area or at the lapel, in the chest area. Uke should grab the side nearest to him or her, making the opening stance gyaku-hanmi. Nage should keep in mind that as in the katatetori attacks, she or he must be ready for Uke's next attack. This makes the initial movement extremely important.

# Katatori Nikkyo

Pictures 3 and 3a show Nage's immediate initial movement. Nage draws the left foot (the foot on the side Uke is grabbing) diagonally back, far enough to stretch Uke's right arm. At this time Nage can apply atemi to Uke's face with his or her right fist (picture 4).

As shown in pictures 3 and 3a, Nage's position after the initial movement should be back far enough so that Uke's left hand cannot reach Nage. As soon as Nage delivers atemi, her or his right hand grabs Uke's wrist and twists it. Pictures 5, 5a, 6, and 6a show this movement, which, needless to say, must be done quickly. As Nage twists Uke's wrist, Nage's left foot advances to Uke's side while he or she puts his or her left hand on Uke's forearm (picture 7).

In pictures 8 and 9, Nage applies nikkyo on Uke's wrist. The details are shown in illustration 17. While Nage is applying pressure with the left hand, the right-hand hold should be maintained tightly until the final pin.

In picture 9, after Nage puts Uke down on the ground with the nikkyo, Nage is executing the final pin. Remember that Nage still holds Uke's wrist tightly with the right hand, even as she or he places the left hand under Uke's elbow. Nage then exerts pressure through the elbow in order to bring Uke face down on the ground (picture 11). In pictures 12 through 16, you can see the switching process of the final pin.

Nikkyo is one of most painful of the wrist techniques in Aikido, and beginners must pay careful attention when applying it. Please do not resist each other until you get the proper idea of the technique or until your wrists become strong and flexible. Basically, Nage is simply bending Uke's wrist and elbow in the direction in which they bend naturally. Whenever you employ a wrist or joint technique you must use the fingers effectively, keeping them strong and tight, just as you practice on yourself during the wrist warm-up exercises.

1

2

3

3a

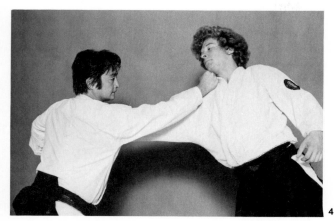

4

6a

5

7

5a

8

6

9

99

10

11

12

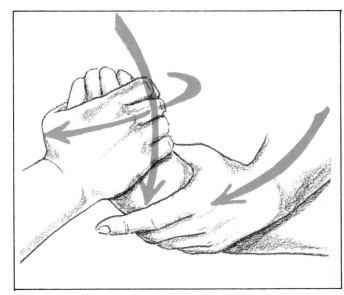

17

13

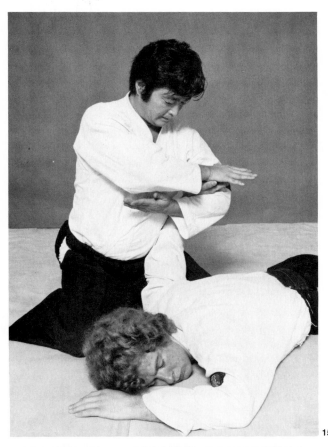

15

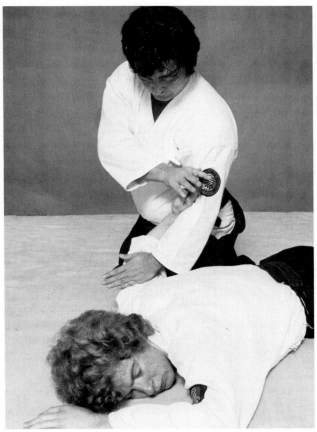

14

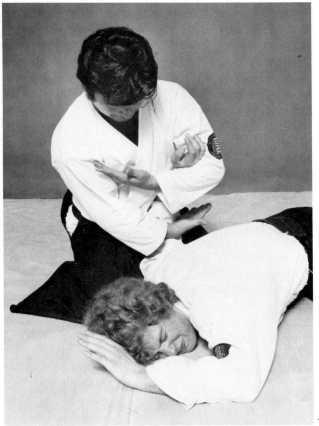

16

# Katatori Yonkyo (Omote)

In this technique all the initial movements are the same as in the previous technique, as seen in pictures 1 through 6. However, at the point at which Nage would have applied the nikkyo, his or her right hand grabs Uke's forearm for the yonkyo form of pressure (pictures 7 and 8). The close-up picture 9 and illustration 18, show the proper way of holding yonkyo.

After Nage switches for the yonkyo with his or her right hand, please notice carefully the way he or she switches the left-hand grab (pictures 9 and 10) in order to maintain more control. After that, Nage keeps applying pressure till Uke is on the ground, as shown in pictures 11, 12, and 13.

In the yonkyo technique Uke's pain doesn't come from pressure against the joints, but rather from pressure received on a nerve point of the forearm. Nage will benefit from executing yonkyo, since it strengthens Nage's holding power.

5

6

7

8

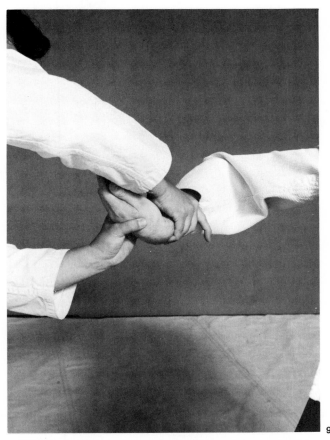

9

10

11

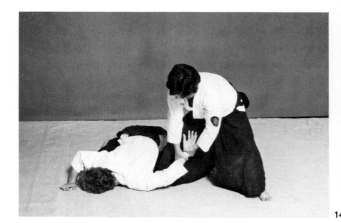

14

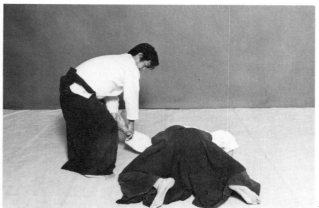

12

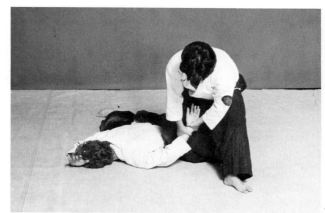

15

13

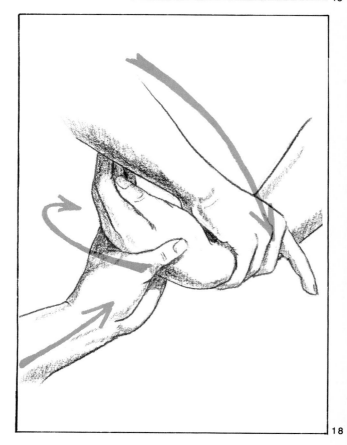

18

# Katetori Menuchi

## The Attack

In the katatori menuchi attack, Uke grabs the sleeve as in katatori and with the other hand strikes shomenuchi (picture 1).

# Katatori Menuchi Irimi Nage

There are two basic ways to initiate movements against this attack. In both, however, it is very important that Nage not stay in the opening position, waiting to receive Uke's attack. Nage should have the attitude of charging forward toward Uke's attack as soon as Uke grabs the sleeve. In order to enter forcefully and not conflict, Nage slides her or his right foot forward (picture 2) to Uke's side while aiming her or his right hand toward Uke's face. This hand motion can be used for either of two purposes: (1) to block Uke's strike or (2) to make Uke block Nage's strike. So occasionally Nage is the one who initiates the entire movement of this technique.

As Nage makes the approach, he or she may be able to overwhelm Uke's strike. If this happens, she or he can do this irimi nage. In picture 3, Nage has obviously overwhelmed Uke, so Nage keeps pressure on Uke's receiving arm. In picture 4, Nage cuts down Uke's arm to Nage's right side. Now he is about to bring his body into the position shown in picture 5. From this point, Nage leads Uke around him as in the basic irimi nage (pictures 6 through 8).

5

6

7

8

# Katatori Menuchi Kotegaeshi

Here again Nage must charge in to meet Uke's attack, rather than to wait for it (pictures 1 and 2). In this case Nage receives Uke's pressure too strongly and cannot overwhelm Uke (picture 3). Now Nage must pivot to get out of Uke's line of attack, as in picture 4. This allows Uke to keep from coming forward and completing the attack. Because of the initial thrust by Nage, combined with the tenkan motion, Uke sometimes loses balance owing to the force of her or his own agressiveness.

In picture 5, after Nage pivots, he brings his arm down, drawing his right foot back. When Nage does this he or she should keep the right arm strong so that Uke can maintain contact and stay with Nage's movement. Otherwise, Uke will slip off. As Nage guides Uke's arm down, Nage grabs for kotegaeshi with the left hand (picture 6) and completes the technique, as shown in pictures 7, 8, and 9.

The important element to note in this technique is that Nage keeps his or her arms extended strongly during the entire movement. Otherwise, there might be a second in which Uke's pressure will get through Nage's weak arm and Nage will end up losing balance.

5

8

6

9

7

# Katatori Menuchi Nikkyo

The movement is the same as that in the kotegaeshi up to the point where Nage goes for Uke's wrist (pictures 1 through 7). Instead of grabbing Uke's striking hand, Nage's left hand grabs the hand that is grabbing at her or his sleeve (picture 8). Nage then applies nikkyo, as shown in pictures 9, 10, and 11.

It will help Nage's movement in the nikkyo technique if he or she continues the motion of the right arm in a full circle, even after guiding Uke's striking arm downward.

5

8

6

9

7

10

11

# Ushiro Ryokatatori

## The Attack

In this attack, Uke grabs both of Nage's shoulders from behind, as shown in picture 1.

# Ushiro Ryokatatori Kotegaeshi

At this point I would like to demonstrate various techniques against attacks from behind Nage's back. It is important for Nage to realize that to apply any kind of technique from a rear attack, Nage must not grab Uke right away. She or he must try to get the best and strongest position first; otherwise, Nage can easily lose balance, making it simple for Uke to get control.

This prinicple holds true in the following technique. Nage is going to grab Uke's wrist for kotegaeshi by getting into a postion that is advantageous not only for kotegaeshi, but for any number of techniques.

In the opening movement, Nage first moves the left foot to the side and at the same time draws the right foot back, turning his or her body in the direction in which his or her right foot is moving (pictures 1 through 4). Please notice the movement of Nage's arms along with the footwork. Nage positions his or her arms in a circle, keeping them that way throughout the movement so that his or her left hand will naturally and automatically reach Uke's wrist for kotegaeshi.

Picture 4 shows exactly what I meant before concerning Nage's attitude in all attacks from behind. You see Nage in a perfect, well-balanced position, enabling him to apply any kind of technique. In this position Nage has Uke off-balance as well.

The movement shown in pictures 4, 5, and 6 should be done very quickly. Picture 6 shows the in-between movement. Nage appears to have stopped there, but he should not do so; the movement must be continuous. If Nage is too anxious to grab Uke's wrist, she or he will end up in this position and be stopped just as is shown in picture 5. After the ideal position is reached, Nage grabs Uke's wrist for kotegaeshi and completes the technique (pictures 6 through 9).

5

8

6

9

7

# Ushiro Ryokatatori Nikkyo (Omote)

Nage's initial movement is the same as in the previous technique (pictures 1, 2, and 3). In this case Nage will step to the right side. Needless to say, the steps shown in pictures 2 and 3 should be done quickly. After Nage gets into position, as in picture 4, he or she grabs Uke's elbow first (the one right in front of Nage), stopping Uke's recovery. With his right hand, Nage grabs Uke's wrist in the nikkyo grab (picture 5), thumb to thumb, with pressure applied to the wrist. After Nage completes the holding position (picture 6), she or he simply moves forward, putting pressure down on Uke's elbow (pictures 7 and 8). After Uke is down on the mat (picture 9), Nage maintains the same hold and puts extra pressure on the wrist, as shown in pictures 10 and 11.

Again Nage should always be trying to get into position (pictures 3 and 4) before trying to grab for the wrist or elbow.

5

9

6

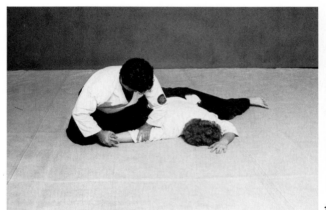

10

7

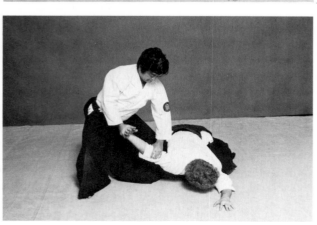

8

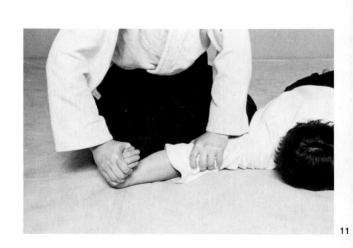

11

# Ushiro Tekubitori

## The Attack

In this attack Uke grabs both of Nage's wrists with both of his hands from behind, as shown in picture 1.

# Ushiro Tekubitori Kotegaeshi

Uke grabs Nage's wrists from behind (picture 1). Nage must now expect that Uke might pull back his or her arms as soon as Nage grabs. To avoid this, Nage should lower her or his weight and bend the wrists forward (picture 2), fingers pointing up, in order to extend Nage's power. This will also serve to join both powers together. Nage should never attempt to move forward before moving his or her arms.

In picture 2, Nage is about to move his arms. Please notice how low Uke's balance is and how Nage's lower body remains centered while his torso avoids leaning forward. If Nage attempts to lift his arms straight up from the sides, Uke can stop him easily. He must first move forward with his arms and then lift up, twisting his arms so that the palms face down at the completion of the arm lift, as shown in picture 6.

From the position in picture 3, Nage makes the exact same movement for kotegaeshi as in ushiro katatori. However, Nage should extend his or her arms fully throughout the entire movement, because Uke is still grabbing both wrists.

In picture 4, Nage brings the left foot back. Here she or he must be sure to step big, the bigger the better. At the same time Nage also moves the left arm in the same direction the left foot is going (picture 5). This will straighten out Uke's arm, making it easy to apply kotegaeshi on that wrist (pictures 6, 7, and 8). Nage should never pull his or her left arm inward as he or he she steps back.

In this technique, once Nage lifts her or his arms up, she or he should always keep both arms in front during the entire movement.

5

7

6

8

# Ushiro Tekubitori Shihonage

The initial movements (pictures 1 through 4) are the same as in the previous technique. If Nage were to do kotegaeshi from the point of picture 5, he or she would bring the left hand down to Uke's wrist. For shihonage, Nage grabs Uke's right wrist with the right hand, putting the right palm inside Uke's wrist. Then Nage's left hand reaches down to meet the right, in order to grab for shihonage.

Nage's arms must always move together continuously (pictures 4, 5, and 6). Picture 6 shows the completion of Nage's grab for shihonage. From that point, Nage lifts both her or his arms and Uke's arm diagonally to Nage's right, with full extension, to throw in shihonage (pictures 7, 8, and 9).

Please notice how in picture 7 Nage strongly stretches or swings Uke's arm using the motion of the entire body. This gives Nage plenty of room to complete the movements.

5

8

6

9

7

121

# Ushiro Tekubitori Sankyo (Omote)

In order for Nage to grab for the sankyo technique, he or she must keep both arms in front of his or her face while making the initial movement (pictures 1, 2, and 3). Uke's left wrist is ready for Nage to grab in sankyo, and Nage's right hand is consequently in the ready position to do the grabbing (picture 4). This happens only if Nage keeps her or his arms fully extended. After Nage grabs for sankyo, as shown in picture 5, he or she can follow the rest of the movements easily, as shown in pictures 6 through 15. Details of the sankyo technique have been described earlier in the book in the shomenuchi sankyo technique. The proper pin position is shown in picture 16.

13

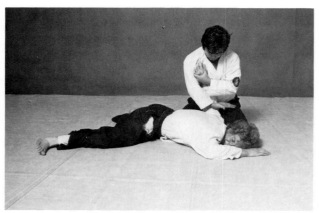

14

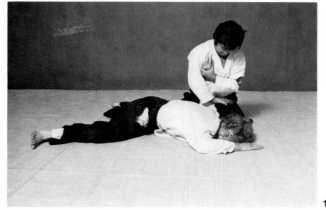

15

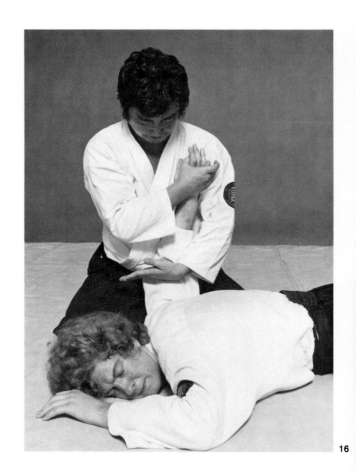

16

# Ushiro Kubishime

## The Attack

In this attack from behind, Uke grabs Nage's wrist with one hand and then applies a choke with the other arm.

# Ushiro Kubishime Koshinage

Nage should pull his or her chin down to stop further choking. Nage can also use her or his free hand to hold Uke's choking arm. Since Uke is choking, Nage cannot move out to the left side (as shown). Everything must be done on his or her right side.

Nage raises the right arm in the same manner as was done in ushiro tekubitori (picture 2). From picture 2 to picture 3 a lot of movement is involved, so please pay particular attention to the arrows in illustration 19, which clearly show the proper direction of movement for Nage's arms and body. First Nage twists her or his body. Next she or he swings the right arm straight down in order to bring Uke over her or his back, as shown in picture 4. At that point, when Uke is on Nage's back, Nage's knees should be bent equally in order to maintain balance. As Nage flips Uke over, Nage should straighten the knees to help lift Uke up.

5

7

6

19

# Ushiro Kubishime Ikkyo (omote)

After Nage brings his or her right arm up in the initial movement (pictures 1 and 2), he or she draws the left foot way back diagonally, extending and stretching his or her right arm completely (picture 3 and 4). In picture 5, Nage grabs Uke's elbow immediately and with the right hand grabs Uke's wrist in the ikkyo technique, as shown in picture 6. From there Nage finishes the ikkyo omote (pictures 7 through 9) as has been shown in previous techniques.

1

2

3

4

5

6

7

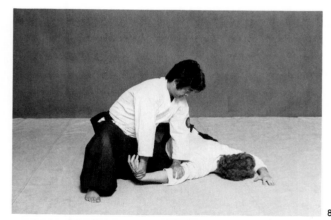

8

9

# Suwari Waza

As students advance in their Aikido practice, they train for many of the techniques in the sitting, or suwari waza, position.

# Suwari Waza Shomenuchi Ikkyo (Omote)

In this demonstration Nage and Uke are in the suwari waza position and Nage will apply ikkyo against the shomenuchi attack (pictures 1 through 6). Refer to the standing shomenuchi ikkyo for the details, substituting the knees for the the feet in the description of footwork.

Since suwari waza is considered to be an advanced level of practice, Nage may feel some difficulty in her or his movements. However, practicing in the sitting position will be of tremendous help when Nage stands to do the technique. This is because when you are sitting, your source of power is limited, and you learn to depend on the center of your energy, the stomach and hips.

3

4

1

5

2

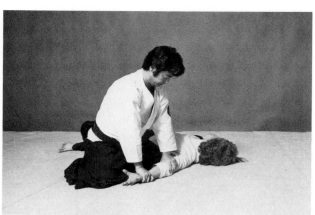

6    131

# Suwari Waza Katatori Nikkyo (Omote)

This movement is the same as that for standing katatori nikkyo, except that Nage must make a bigger initial movement. The grab for the wrist is the same as in nikkyo ura (picture 5) except that instead of turning, Nage continues forward (picture 6) as in the ikkyo technique shown in ushiro kubishime. Nage finishes the technique with nikkyo pressure on the wrist (pictures 7 and 8).

5

7

6

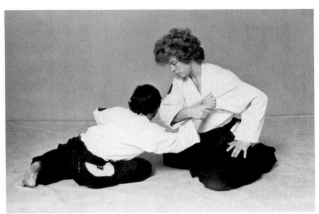

8

# Hanmi Handachi

## The Attack

For further advanced practice, Nage stays in the sitting position while Uke attacks from a standing postion (picture 1.)

# Katatetori Shihonage
# (Hanmi Handachi)

The entire movement is the same as that of standing katatetori shihonage. Once again, since Nage is in a sitting position, he or she must make the movement bigger and wider than if standing. In picture 1, Nage should be expecting Uke's right-hand attack after the grab, so Nage must make the initial movement (picture 2) very quickly. Nage advances with the left knee, lifting up her or his arm to cover and protect his or her face, as in picture 3. This movement also serves to break Uke's balance. Pictures 4, 5, and 6 complete the technique.

3

4

1

5

2

6  135

# Katatetori Uchi Kaitenage (Hanmi Handachi)

In this technique Nage's initial movement must again be immediate. Here Nage extends the right arm out to the side, advancing on his or her right knee, as shown in picture 2. At that time, Nage applies atemi with a fist or elbow to Uke's belly (picture 3). Nage then brings her or his body under Uke's left arm and pivots, as in pictures 3 and 4. During that time Nage should keep extending the right arm strongly.

Picture 4 shows Nage's completed pivot. From there, Nage swings the arm down, drawing his or her right knee way back in order to bring Uke's head down in front of him or her (picture 5). To complete the throw, Nage puts the left hand on the back of Uke's head and pushes down while at the same time the right hand grabs Uke's left wrist (picture 6) and pushes forward on Uke's arm (picture 7).

5

7

6

# Katatetori Soto Kaitenage (Hanmi Handachi)

As in the last technique, when Nage makes the initial movement, instead of going under Uke's arm, she or he turns on the outside of Uke's body, circling, her or his arm in front of her or his face, as seen in pictures 2 through 4. As Nage circles the arm, Nage should bend the elbow slightly instead of giving a full extension. Picture 4 shows the completion of the outside pivot, when Nage should resume extension of the right arm. From there, Nage swings his or her arm down on a slight diagonal, drawing the left knee back in order to bring Uke's head down and in front of him or her (picture 5). The rest of the throw is the same as in the previous kaitenage (pictures 6 and 7).

1

2

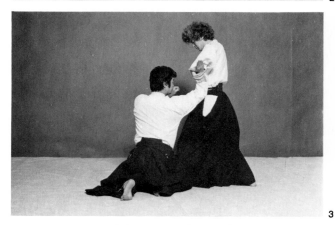

3

4

**5**

**7**

**6**

# Advanced Techniques

The following techniques are easily developed from the various attacks used before in the basic techniques.

In these techniques you will notice how important the initial movement is against any attack. After the intial movement is performed perfectly, one can apply countless techniques against each attack.

Also please remember to always get your position first. A better position is more important than the technique. If you are only aiming for certain grabs or holds, your entire movement will be limited, and you will sometimes find that Uke is in a better and more balanced position than yours. Actually, once Uke's balance is broken, Nage can throw Uke without any effort or technique.

6

7

8

9

*143*

# Yokomenuchi Koshinage

7

5

8

6

145

# Shomenuchi Shihonage

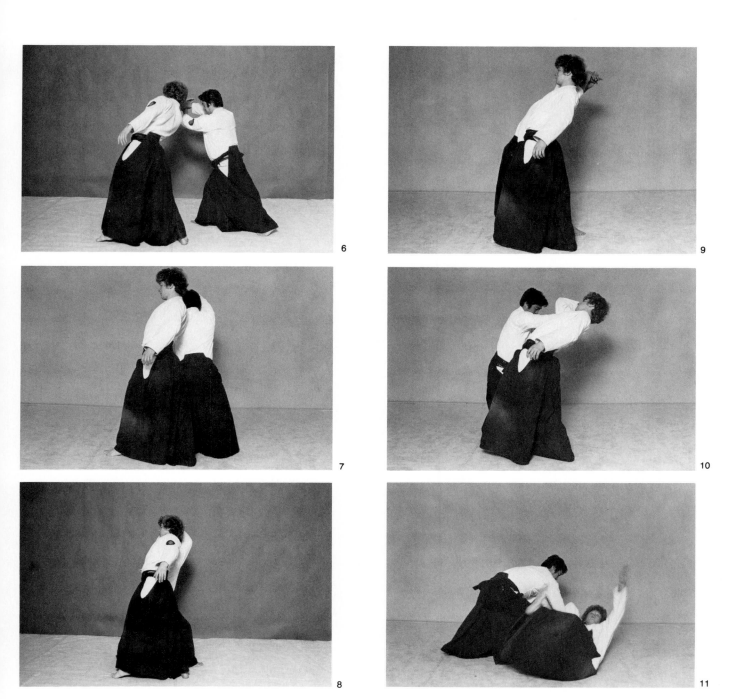

6

7

8

9

10

11

# Shomenuchi Udekimenage

4

1

5

2

3

148

6

7

8

9

149

# Shomenuchi Koshinage

5

6

7

8

# Shomenuchi Kokyunage

1

2

3

4

5

6

9

7

10

8

153

# Ryotetori Koshinage

1

2

3

5

6

7

154

# Ryotetori Kokyunage

1

2

3

4

5

6

# Ryotetori Kokyunage

4

1

5

2

6

3

# Tsuki Kaitennage

1

2

3

4

5

# Ushiro Tekubitori Koshinage

1

2

3

4

5

6

9

7

10

8

159

# Ushiro Tekubitori Jujinage

5

6

7

8

# Techniques Against Weapons

The following demonstrations will show how to apply Aikido techniques against weapons such as the knife (tanto), wooden sword (boken), and stick (jo). Needless to say, before you can apply these techniques you must have a great deal of experience and practice in the basics.

Because weapons are involved, Nage's mental attitude is the most important aspect of these techniques. Nage must consider her or his opponent as not having a weapon. If you are conscious of the weapon and focus your attention on it, your movement will be limited.

Nage must keep the same attitude as during the basic empty-handed techniques. For example, although you may have been practicing for ten years, if your mental attitude is easily upset or you become frightened when you see your opponent with a weapon, your body cannot apply *any* technique. That is why in our daily training we try to maintain a relaxed and calm manner throughout our entire practice.

4

1

2

5

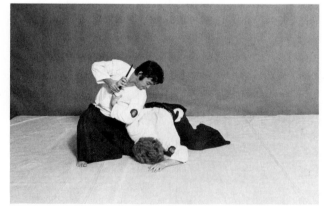

6

3

*163*

10

7

11

8

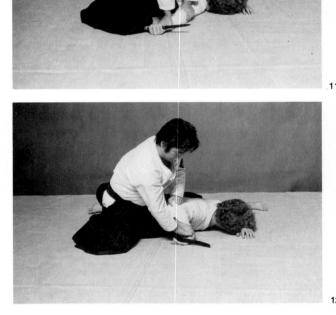

12

9

16

13

17

14

18

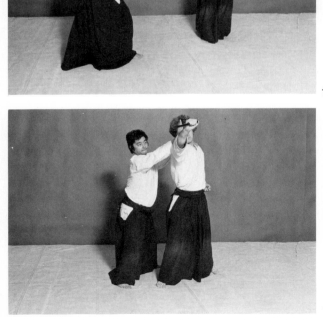

15

165

22

19

23

20

24

21

25

26

27

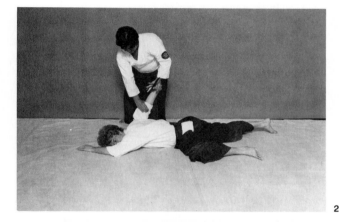

28

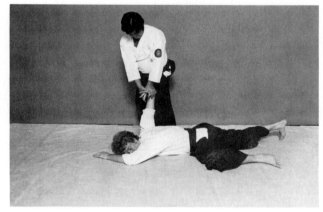

29

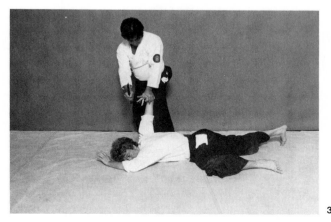

30 *167*

1

2

3

4

7

5

8

6

9

10

11

12

13

14

15

170

19

16

20

17

21

18

171

23

24

25

27

26

173

31

28

32

29

33

30

34

35

36

37

38

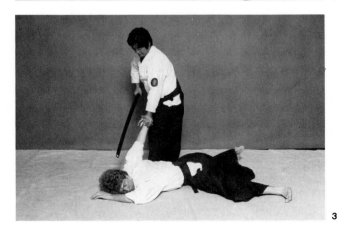

39

175

43

40

44

41

42

45

46

47

48

177

3

1

4

2

5

6

7

8

12

9

13

10

14

11

18

15

19

16

20

17

*181*

24

21

25

22

26

182

23

27

# Action Photos

This series of pictures shows more clearly the continuous movement in Aikido. You can see how Nage keeps Uke's movement or attack going, nonstop. This makes Uke lose balance through his or her own momentum. You should also notice how Nage always moves into Uke's shikaku and leads Uke around in a circular manner so that Nage actually requires less movement than Uke. Also notice that during the entire movement Nage is always extending his power out. This serves to keep the momentum going.

# Ushiro Kubishime Iriminage

# Morotetori Jujinage

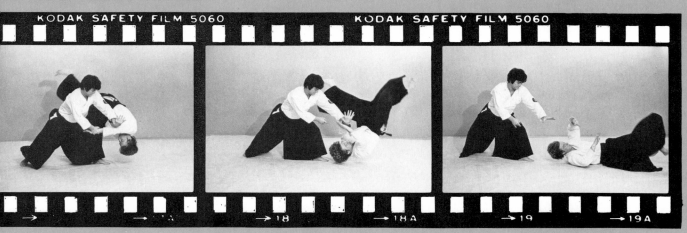

# Ryokatatori Iriminage

189

# Tsuki Iriminage

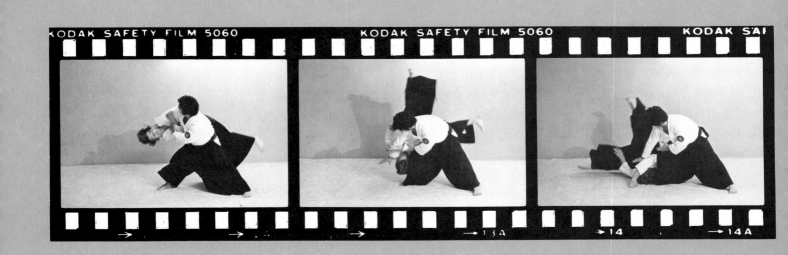

# Yokomenuchi Kokyunage

# Yokomenuchi Iriminage

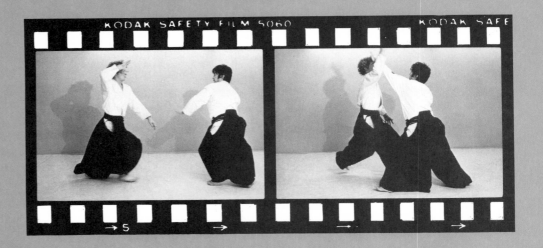

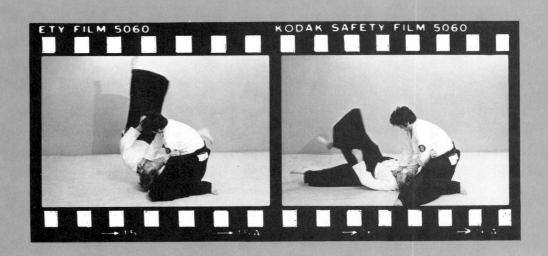

# Aiki Otoshi

# Two-man Attack - Kokyunage

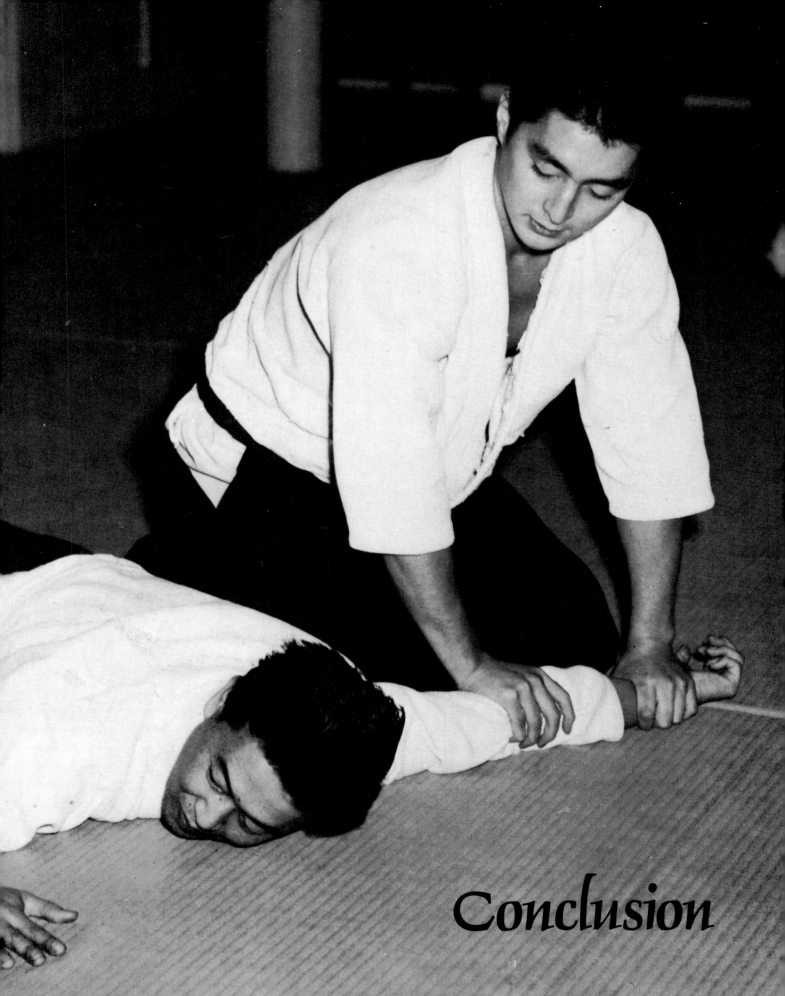

Conclusion

All the techniques I have demonstrated in this book consist of the basic movements and skills. Thousands of other techniques can be applied, depending on the type and nature of the attack. Sometimes it is impossible to show techniques through still photography, owing to the nature of the Aikido movement, which is very flexible, continuous, and circular. However, there is a very concrete aspect of Aikido which can be gained through daily practice: the development of a healthy mental attitude. The confidence and self-control that can be built go hand in hand with technical growth. This is why martial-arts training is a lifelong pursuit. There is no limit, no end to what you can develop through practice. The more you practice the more there is to gain and the deeper the meanings you can glean.

I believe that truly strong people do not get involved in fighting. One should be able to reach that stage of development after a long training period. Only through that process can one discover that the real winner is the one who never fights. That should be the ultimate goal of the martial artist.

I would be more than happy if this book contributes to the understanding and introduction of the art of Aikido for those who were not familiar with it before. For those who are already involved in Aikido, I hope the book will serve as a guide for their further study and prove beneficial in their daily practice.

\*     \*     \*

There are many qualified instructors of Aikido in the United States. I'd like to suggest that you seek their instruction at some point in your Aikido study.

It is my sincere hope that through the principles of Aikido, which are the concepts of nonfighting and unity of movement, all people will be able to learn to live in harmony with each other and the world.

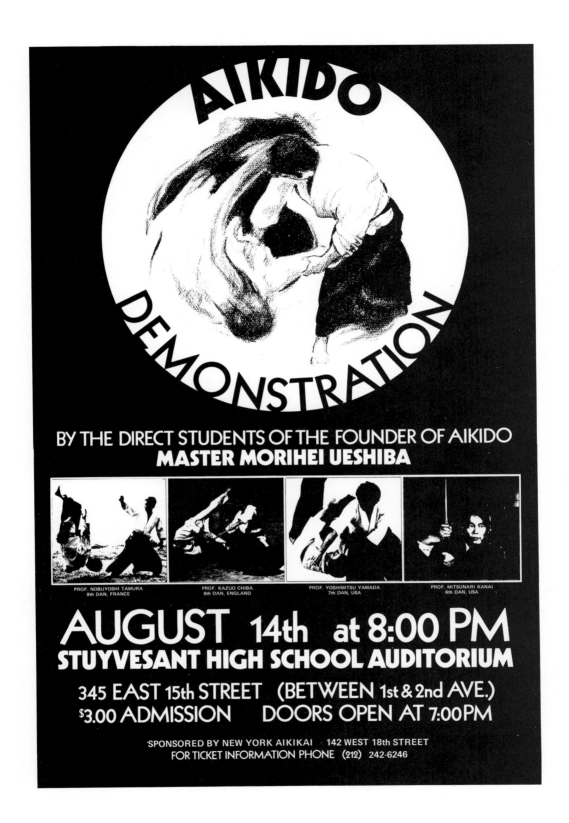

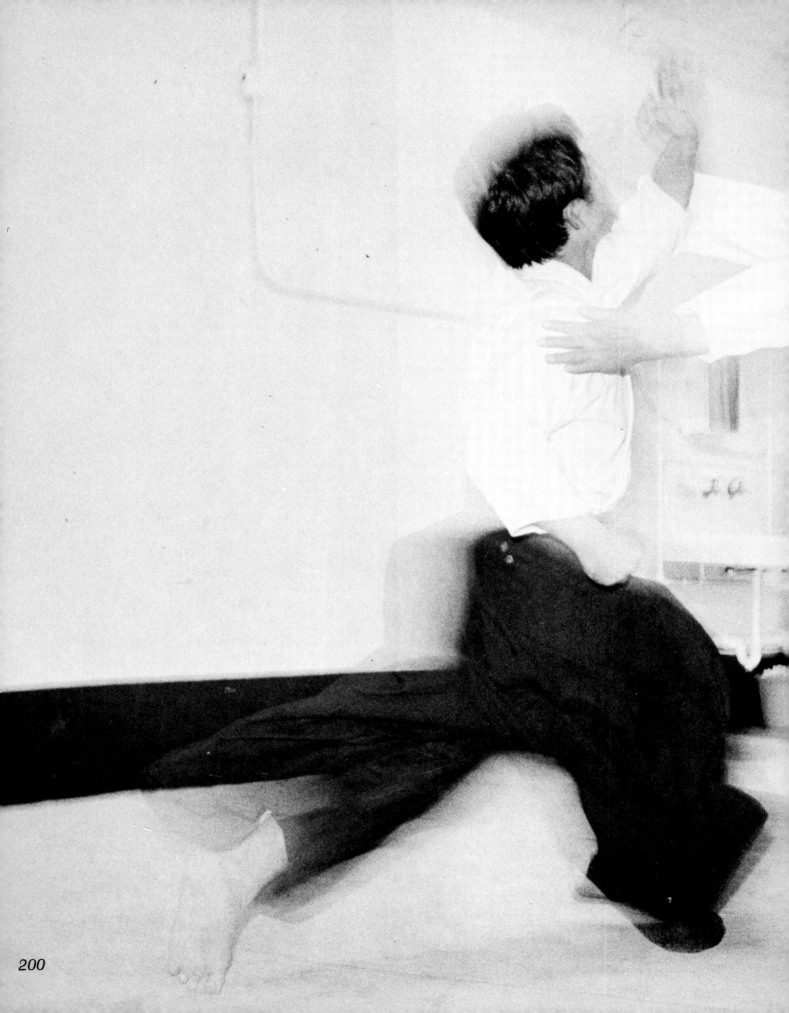

# The International Aikido Community & Dojo Listings

# International Aikido Federation

It was the wish of Aikido founder Morihei Ueshiba that Aikido should serve to benefit all people and that the family of Aikidoists throughout the world should unite to help achieve this ideal. In light of his desires, the Aikikai Foundation, with its home at Aikido World Headquarters in Tokyo, was formed to assure that these desires would become reality. At the request of the Aikikai Foundation, delegates from those countries with established Aikido programs convened in Tokyo, so that by 1975 the International Aikido Federation (IAF) was established, with Doshu Kisshomaru Ueshiba elected president for life. It was decided that in order to clarify the communications between the world Aikido community and the Aikikai Foundation, each nation was to have one national federation as its official representative to the IAF.

## INTERNATIONAL DOJO DIRECTORY

### ARGENTINA

T. Kurata
Crel Aplinanio Figuero 101, Cap Fed, Argentina

K. Miyazawa, Instituto Argentino de Aikido
Triunvirato 4326/38, Local 18, Cap Fed, Argentina

### BRAZIL

Dr. R. Kawai, Brazil Aikikai
Rue Clovis Rosa Da Silva 31, CEP 05530
Previdencia, Sao Paulo, Brazil

### CANADA

Canadian Aikido Federation, W. Collins, President
Toronto Aikikai, 260 Richmond St. West, 3rd floor
Toronto, Ontario, Canada

Y. Kawahara, Vancouver Aikikai, 62E Cordova St.
Vancouver, British Columbia, V6A 1K2, Canada

Dr. M. Langford, Newfoundland Aikikai, 7 Wickham Place
St. John's, Newfoundland, Canada

O. Obata, Japanese Canadian Cultural Center,
Box 191, 123 Wynford Dr.
Don Mills, Ontario, M3C 2S2, Canada

M. N. DiVilladorata, Montreal Aikikai
4510 St. Denis, Montreal, Quebec, Canada

### CHILE

Chile Aikikai, Dr. Julio Ponce Z, Calle Latorre 201
La Calera, Chile

### EUROPE

European Aikido Federation, P. Chassang, General Secretary
31 Rue de Mimont, 06400 Cannes, France

Austria: J. Iwamoto, Austria Aikido Federation
6 Wien, Munzwardeing 3-1, Austria

J. Yoshida, Hoher Markt 8-9/2/28, A-1010 Wien Austria

Belgium: Belgium Aikido Federation, J. Byllos, General Secretary
Rue Virgile 51, 1070 Bruxelles, Belgium

Denmark: N. Bodker, Copenhagen Aikikai
Rundorbiveji 69b, 2950 Vedb K, Denmark

Finland: H. Strommer, Finland Aikikai
Ylioppilaskyla 5 C 1, 20510, Turku 51, Finland

France: T. Suga, 31 Rue de Clery, 75002, Paris, France

N. Tamura, Chemin des 4 Platanes
83470 St. Maximin, France

Great Britain: M. Kanetsuka, British Aikido Federation
38 Hillfield Road, London NW6 1PZ, England

Greece: C. Politis, Greece Aikido Federation, 149 Patisson St.
Athens 814, Greece

Holland: J. J. Brakel, Budo Bond Nederland
Iaan Van Meerdervoort 239, Den Haag, Holland

Ireland: M. Brennan, Ireland Aikikai,
4 Upper Fitzwilliam St., Dublin 2, Ireland

Italy: F. Fujimoto, Via Cenisio 76-5, Milano 00185, Italy

Luxembourg: Pe'l Schlechter, Case Postale 110, Luxembourg

Morocco: M. Benomar, Aikido Section of the Morocco Judo Fed.
Parc de la Ligue Arabe, A'Casablanca, Morocco

Spain: Y. Kitaura, Andres Mellada 46 D, Madrid 15, Spain

Mr. Pulida, Aikido Section of Spanish Judo Fed.
Hortaleza 108, Madrid 4, Spain

Sweden: T. Ichimura, Sweden Aikikai,
c/o Westh Lanhomsgatan IA N 117
33 Stockholm, Sweden

T. Tomida, Aikido Dojo Stockholm, Kommendorsgatan 29, 114
48 Stockholm, Sweden

Switzerland: M. Ikeda, Klaraweg 12, 3006 Bern, Switzerland

H. Jilli, Swiss Aikikai, Qoerstr 9, 8050 Zurich, Switzerland

West Germany: K. Asai, 4 Dusseldorf, Helmholtzstr 20, West Germany

### HONG KONG

Wong Sui Shing, Hong Kong Aikido Association
929 Wah Shun Hoose Wah Estate, Hong Kong

### INDONESIA

J. M. Parawira Widjaya, Surabaya Aikido Club
Kimbungan 11-No.2B, Surabaya, Indonesia

KOREA

Myung Jal Nan, Korean Aikikai
Iwnchow Chu-Ku, Rue-Tong 9, Republic of Korea

MACAU

Lee Wain Sin, Murayama Aikido
No. 20, 2nd Floor, Travessa dos Santos, Macau

MALAYSIA

J. Yamada, P.O. Box 592, Kuchin, Sarawak, Malaysia

MEXICO

Y. Kurita, Edificio 40-B, No.403, Lomas de Sotelo
Mexico 10 D.F. Mexico

NEW ZEALAND

J. D. Lanham, c/o Otahuhu Police, Auckland, New
Zealand

SINGAPORE

J. C. H. Geow, Metropolitan YMCA Aikido Club
Tanglia Center, 60 Stevens Road, Singapore 10

SOUTH AFRICA

R. Ryan, 21 Saturn Road, Westville 3630, South Africa

TAHITI

M. Brun, Aikikai de Tahiti, P.O. Box 567, Papbete, Tahiti

TAIWAN

Lee Ching Nan, Republic of China Aikido Assoc.
Fl. 8, 309 Tun-Hua Road N., Taipai, Taiwan

THAILAND

M. Fukakusa, Thailand Aikido Association, No. 79
Sai Akkapat Sukumit, Sukumvit Road, Bangkok,
Thailand

URUGUAY

Prof. M. Cela, Uruguay Aikikai, 1320 Montevideo,
Uruguay

UNITED STATES

United States Aikido Federation, 142 West 18th St.
New York, N.Y. 10011, U.S.A.

# United States Aikido Federation

In keeping with the agreements of the IAF congress, I returned to the United States and proceded to contact all dojos and clubs throughout the country, to notify them of the IAF decisions, and to invite them to an organizational meeting in December 1976 at my dojo, the New York Aikikai. During the three days of meetings, the representatives agreed upon the purposes and structure of the fledgling federation. The drafts of the constitution and bylaws were accepted. Amendments to both were added in subsequent congresses.

The United States Aikido Federation (USAF) is set up as a nonprofit organization made up of affiliated dojos and Aikido clubs from all areas of the United States. Its purposes include the development and improvement of Aikido practice in the United States under the guidance of the Aikikai Foundation and its designated representatives. It establishes grading standards and represents the interests of its members to both the IAF and the Aikikai Foundation. The USAF has built up a communication system whereby it fosters the spirit of understanding, friendship, and commitment among its members.

Some of the ways in which these goals have been achieved are the sponsorship of special training camps and seminars throughout the country. These sessions feature visits from the four *shihans* (professors) who teach permanently in the United States and from visiting instructors from Tokyo and around the world. As well as being educational from a technical standpoint, the seminars and camps encourage new friendships, resulting in greater inter-dojo travel, practice, and mutual concern.

Also helping in the area of communication is the official newsletter of the USAF, the *Federation News*. It is published quarterly and features information regarding seminars, camps, trips, demonstrations, and publications, as well as feature articles by teachers and students.

The technical development of the USAF is the responsibility of the Technical Committee. It is their job to set promotion requirements, advise on proper instruction procedures, and generally monitor the standard of practice so that instruction can be directed to areas of training that require immediate attention. Presently the permanent members of the Technical Committee (as approved by Aikido World Headquarters) are Mr. Mitsunari Kanai, 7th Dan from New England, who, with myself, was an original apprentice of O Sensei; Mr. Akira Tohei, 7th Dan from Chicago; and myself, from New York.

The USAF has more than seventy affiliated dojos at this time and is playing an ever-increasing role in serving the needs of the Aikido community both here and abroad.

The United States Aikido Federation Headquarters
142 West 18th Street, New York, N. Y.   10011
(212) 242-6246

## UNITED STATES AFFILIATED DOJOS

ARIZONA

Canyonland Aikido
25 W. Calle Concordia
Tucson, AZ 85704

ARKANSAS

Central Arkansas Aikido
P.O. Box 431
Conway, AR 72032

CALIFORNIA

Aikido-Ai-Southern California
2676 Turnbull Cyn. Road
Hacienda Heights, CA 91745

Aikido Club of Berkeley
1407 San Pablo Ave.
Berkeley, CA 94702

Aikido Institute
6048 College Ave.
Oakland, CA 94618

Aikido of San Francisco
678 Turk St.
San Francisco, CA 94102

Aikido West
3410 Devon Way
Redwood City, CA 94061

Aikikai of Tahoe
Box 5521
Tahoe City, CA 95730

Alhambra Aikikai
1928 W. Valley Blvd.
Alhambra, CA 91801

Beverly Hills Aikido Club
8233 West 3rd St.
West Hollywood, CA 90048

Hollywood Aikido Club
1146 North Vermont Ave.
Hollywood, CA 90029

Los Angeles Aikikai
8929 Ellis Ave.
Los Angeles, CA 90034

Pasadena Aikikai
595 N. Lincoln Ave.
Pasadena, CA 91103

Sacramento Aikikai
4111-B Power Inn Road
Sacramento, CA 95826

San Francisco Aikikai
1632 Alabama St.
San Francisco, CA 94110

Stockton Aikido Club
2648 Palo Vista Way
Rancho Cordova, CA 95670

Ventura Aikikai
6868 Dove St.
Ventura, CA 93003

West Los Angeles Aikido Institute
1543 Sawtelle Blvd.
Los Angeles, CA 90025

TRW Aikido Club
R2/2036 1 Space Park
Redondo Beach, CA 90278

CONNECTICUT

Aikikai of Southwestern Connecticut
268 Dogwood Lane
Stamford, CT 06903

Wesleyan Aikido Club
    Dept. of Theatre
190 High Street
Middletown, CT 06457

Aikikai of Guilford
841 West Lake Ave.
Guilford, CT 06437

FLORIDA

Florida Aikikai
35 S.W. 1st Ave.
Dania, FL 33004

Gainesville Aikikai
c/o Robert Ho, 2200 NE 7 St.
Gainesville, FL 32601

Miami Aikikai
2621 S.W. 37th Ave.
Coral Gables, FL 33133

Sand Drift School of Aikido
312 Palm Ave.
Titusville, FL 32730

Tallahassee Aikikai Shurin-Dojo
607-18 Dixie Dr.
Tallahassee, FL 32304

GEORGIA

Aikido Center of Atlanta
c/o R. Grantham,
3724 Wassaw Lane
Duluth, GA 30136

HAWAII

Hawaii Aiki Kwai
3224 Waialae Ave.
Honolulu, HA 96816

ILLINOIS

Midwest Aikido Center
3943 N. Lincoln Ave.
Chicago, IL 60613

Glen Ellyn Aikido Club
c/o ALU-College of DuPage
Glen Ellyn, IL 60137

Illini Aikido Club
410 E. Michigan #2
Urbana, IL 61801

Northern Illinois Univ. Aikido Club
Northern Illinois University
Dekalb, IL 60115

IOWA

Iowa Aikikai
7600 Dennis Drive #13
Urbandale, IA 50322

MARYLAND

Baltimore Aikikai
    Harford Com College
401 Thomas Run Road
Bel Air, MD 21014

MASSACHUSETTS

New England Aikikai
2000 Mass Ave.
Cambridge, MA 02140

Andover Aikido
10 Brook St.
Andover, MA 01810

Newburyport Aikido
YMCA 96 State St.
Newburyport, MA 01950

Nonotuck Aikikai
P.O. Box 115
Florence, MA 01060

Northeast Aikikai
265 Dutton St.
Lowell, MA 01852

Shodokan
438 Humphrey St.
Swampscott, MA 01907

Tonan Judo Club
109 Worcester St.
New Bedford, MA 02745

University of Mass. Aikikai
c/o T. Unno, 89 Marian St.
Northampton, MA 01060

MINNESOTA

Twin Cities Aikido Center &
    Univ. of Minnesota Aikido Club
2390 University Ave.
St. Paul, MN 55114

MISSOURI

Ai Shin Kan Aikido School
4006 E. 104th St.
Kansas City, MO 64137

MONTANA

Univ. of Montana Aikido Club
130 D. Buena Vista Court
Missoula, MT 59801

NEW JERSEY

Dutch Neck Aikikai
P.O. Box 94
Greenwich, NJ 08323

South Jersey Aikikai
124 W. Indiana Ave.
Beach Haven Terrace, NJ 08008

Stockton Aikido Club
Stockton State College
Pomona, NJ 08240

Union County Aikikai
1156 E. Jersey St.
Elizabeth, NJ 07201

NEW MEXICO

Albuquerque Aikido Dojo
206 San Mateo S.E.
Albuquerque, NM 87108

NEW YORK

New York Aikikai
142 West 18th St.
New York, NY 10011

Brooklyn Aikido Club
P.O. Box 222
Brooklyn, NY 11207

Cantine's Island Aikikai
P.O. Box 334
Saugerties, NY 12477

Central New York Aikikai
2363 James St.
Syracuse, NY 13206

Long Island Aikido Assoc.
303 Maple Ave.
Rockville Centre, NY 11570

OHIO

Cincinnati Aikikai
270 Southern Ave.
Cincinnati, OH 45219

Cleveland Aikikai
7305 Lakeshore Blvd.
Cleveland, OH 44060

Youngstown Aikikai
2705 Market St.
Youngstown, OH 44507

PENNSYLVANIA

New Castle Aikikai
215 Taylor St.
New Castle, PA 06101

Pittsburgh Aikikai
5931 Penn Mall
Pittsburgh, PA 15206

RHODE ISLAND

Rhode Island Aikikai
YMCA 160 Broad St.
Providence, RI

SOUTH CAROLINA

Mt. Pleasant Aikido
c/o J. Simon, 7 Lauden St.
Isle of Palms, SC 29451

VERMONT

Vermont Aikikai
YMCA 266 College St.
Burlington, VT 05401

WASHINGTON

Seattle School of Aikido
3422 N.E. 55th
Seattle, WA 98115

Washington Aiki Kwai
22406 53 W.
Mountlake Terrace, WA 98043

WASHINGTON D.C.

Capital Aikikai
5809 Osceola Rd.
Bethesda, MD 20016

WISCONSIN

Madison Aikido Club,
YWCA 101 East Mifflin St.
Madison, WI 53703

Milwaukee Aikido Club
4723 West Center St.
Milwaukee, WI 53210

Univ. of Wisconsin Aikido Club
4317 Clover Ct.
Madison, WI 53711

Wausau Aikido Club
YMCA, 707 Third St.
Wausau, WI 54401

Glossary

**Ai-hanmi:** when the partners are facing each other in a mutual triangular stance.

**Aikikai:** the name of any aikido school recognized by Aikido World Headquarters.

**Atemi:** the use of striking techniques.

**Boken:** *see* Tachi, boken.

**Budo:** any Japanese martial art.

**Dojo:** a place where martial arts training takes place.

**Doshu:** the title of the present leader of Aikido.

**Eritori:** an attack in which the collar is grabbed from behind.

**Gi:** practice uniform.

**Gokkyo:** one of the wrist techniques in which the wrist is held palm up; usually employed against a knife attack.

**Gyaku-hanmi:** the partners stand in opposite triangular stances.

**Hanmi:** a triangular stance, the basic on-guard position.

**Hanmi handachi:** Nage is in a sitting posture and Uke attacks from a standing posture.

**Ikkyo:** a wrist technique where the arm is held without applying pressure to the joints.

**Irimi, tenkan:** basic opening movements in Aikido techniques. Irimi is a motion in which one charges directly towards the opponent; tenkan is a motion in which one turns or pivots away from the opponent.

**Irimi nage:** a throwing technique employing an "entering" motion.

**Jo:** wooden staff.

**Jo tori:** technique applied against attack with a jo.

**Juji nage:** a type of throw in which Nage uses the pressure of crossing Uke's arms against each other.

**Kaitenage:** a throw in which Nage employs a spinning motion to throw Uke forward; pressure is exerted by holding Uke's head down and pushing the arm on a diagonal.

**Katatetori:** an attack in which Uke grabs one of Nage's hands in one of his or her hands.

**Katatori:** an attack in which Uke grabs at Nage's lapel or shoulder.

**Ki:** inner energy based on calmness.

**Kokyu-ho, kokyu-ryoku:** kokyu-ryoku is breath power emanating from the abdomen; kokyu-ho is a method of coordinating breath power and body movement to increase one's ki power.

**Kokyu nage:** a type of throw employing no joint technique.

**Kokyu-ryoku:** *see* kokyu-ho, kokyu-ryoku.

**Koshinage:** a throw in which Uke is thrown over Nage's hips.

**Kotegaeshi:** one of the wrist techniques in which pressure is applied on the wrist away from Uke's body.

**Morotetori:** an attack in which Uke grabs Nage's forearm with both hands.

**Maai:** the proper distance beween Uke and Nage.

**Nage:** the partner executing the technique.

**Nikkyo:** one of the wrist techniques in which pressure is applied on the wrist toward Uke's body.

**Omote, ura:** the description of Nage's position in executing the techniques. Omote is based on irimi movements and is done going toward Uke; ura is based on tenkan movements making Uke move around Nage.

**Osae:** a pin, a method of holding down.

**O Sensei:** Morihei Ueshiba, the founder of Aikido.

**Rei, ojigi:** proper bowing.

**Reigi:** etiquette.

**Ryotetori:** an attack in which Uke grabs both of Nage's wrists in both of his or her hands.

**Sankyo:** one of the wrist techniques in which pressure is applied against the wrist in a twisting motion toward Uke.

**Seiza:** proper sitting.

**Shihonage:** a technique in which pressure is applied against Uke's wrist and elbow using a sword-swinging motion to throw Uke down.

**Shikko:** a technique of walking on the knees.

**Shomenuchi:** an attack in which Uke strikes at Nage's forehead with an open hand.

**Soto kaiten:** an outside turning motion.

**Suwari waza:** techniques, done from a sitting position, in which Uke and Nage employ shikko.

**Tachi, boken:** a wooden sword.

**Tachi tori:** techniques applied against attacks with a boken.

**Tachi waza:** techniques done with Uke and Nage standing.

**Tanto:** a wooden knife.

**Tanto tori:** techniques applied against knife attacks.

**Tenchi nage:** a type of irimi nage in which Nage breaks Uke's balance by extending one hand up and the other down while moving toward Uke.

**Tenkan:** *see* Irimi, tenkan.

**Uchi katen:** an inside turning motion.

**Udekime nage:** a type of throw applying pressure to the underside of the elbow.

208

**Uke:** the partner initiating the "attack".
**Ukemi:** protective falling.
**Ura:** *see* Omote, ura.
**Ushiro kubishime:** an attack in which Uke grabs one of Nage's wrists from behind and chokes Nage with the other arm.
**Ushiro ryokatatori:** an attack in which Uke grabs Nage's shoulders from behind.
**Ushiro tekubitori:** an attack in which Uke grabs both of Nage's wrists from behind.

**Waza:** technique.

**Yokomenuchi:** an attack in which Uke strikes at the side of Nage's neck or head with an open hand.
**Yonkyo:** a technique in which pressure is applied against Uke's forearm.

**Zen:** a form of meditation based on a Japanese philosophy.

# USAF Promotional Test Requirements

## KYU TESTS

### 5th Kyu (60 hours)
1. Shomenuchi Ikkyo (omote & ura)
2. Shomenuchi Iriminage
3. Katatetori Shihonage (omote & ura)
4. Ryotetori Tenchinage
5. Tsuki Kotegaeshi
6. Ushiro Tekubitori Kotegaeshi
7. Morotetori Kokyuho

### 4th Kyu (80 hours)
1. Shomenuchi Nikkyo (omote & ura)
2. Yokomenuchi Shihonage (omote & ura)
3. Tsuki Iriminage
4. Ushiro Tekubi Sankyo (omote & ura)
5. Ushiro Ryokatatori Kotegaeshi
6. Suwari Waza: Shomenuchi Ikkyo
   Katatori Nikkyo (omote & ura)
   Katatori Sankyo

### 3rd Kyu (100 hours)
1. Yokomenuchi Iriminage (2 ways)
2. Yokomenuchi Kotegaeshi
3. Tsuki Kaitennage
4. Ushiro Ryokatatori Sankyo (omote & ura)
5. Morotetori Iriminage (2 ways)
6. Shomenuchi Sankyo (omote & ura)
7. Suwari Waza: Shomenuchi Iriminage
   Shomenuchi Nikkyo (omote & ura)
8. Hanmi-Handachi: Katatetori Shihonage
   Katatetori Kaitennage
   (uchi & soto mawari*)

### 2nd Kyu (150 hours)
1. Shomenuchi Shihonage
2. Shomenuchi Kaitennage
3. Yokomenuchi Gokyo
4. Ushiro Tekubitori Shihonage
5. Ushiro Tekubitori Jujinage
6. Ushiro Kubishime Koshinage
7. Morotetori Nikkyo
8. Hanmi-Handachi: Shomenuchi Iriminage
   Katatetori Nikkyo
   Yokomenuchi Kotegaeshi
9. Freestyle—2 persons

*Uchi & Soto Mawari—both inside (uchi) and outside (soto) movements

### 1st Kyu (200 hours)
1. Katatori Menuchi—
   5 techniques
2. Yokomenuchi—5 techniques
3. Morotetori—5 techniques
4. Shomenuchi—5 techniques
5. Ryotetori—5 techniques
6. Koshinage—5 techniques
7. Tantotori
8. Hanmi-Handachi (Ushiro Waza—5 techniques)
9. Freestyle—3 persons

## DAN TESTS

### Sho-Dan (300 hours)
1. All of 1st Kyu requirements
2. Tachitori
3. Jotori
4. Henkawaza**
5. Freestyle—4 persons

### Ni-Dan (500 hours)
1. Attend 2 seminars per year after
   Sho-Dan.
2. All of Sho-Dan requirements
3. Tachitori—2
4. Freestyle—5
5. Kaeshiwaza***

### San-Dan (600 hours)
1. Attend 2 seminars per year after Ni-Dan.
   Subject of exam to be determined by
   examiner at the time of the exam.

*Note: Hour requirements are counted from the last test.*

**Henkawaza—switching from one technique to another. Examiner will call the first technique.

***Kaeshiwaza—counter techniques. Uke applies the technique to nage. Original technique will be called by examiner. (e.g. to apply sankyo against nikkyo)